There's a God for That

for that

Optimism in the face of earthquakes, tsunamis and meltdowns

Joseph Honton

Frankalmoigne
Sebastopol, California

Published by Frankalmoigne
Sebastopol, California.

Printed in the United States of America.
Typeface: Adobe Jenson Pro 12/16.

Library of Congress Control Number: 2012940666

Publisher's Cataloging-in-Publication data:
Honton, Joseph, 1958–.
    There's a god for that : optimism in the face of earthquakes, tsunamis and meltdowns / Joseph Honton.
    p. cm.
    ISBN 978-0-9856423-0-3 (hardcover : alk. paper) -- ISBN 978-0-9856423-1-0 (pbk.) -- ISBN 978-0-9856423-2-7 (ePub) -- ISBN 978-0-9856423-3-4 (Mobi)
1. Japan – Religious life and customs. 2. Earthquakes – Japan. 3. Tsunamis – Japan. 4. Fukushima Daiichi Nuclear Power Plant (Japan) – Accidents. 5. Antinuclear movement. 6. Ghost stories, Japanese. I. Title.

BISAC subject headings:
    TRV003050 : TRAVEL / Asia / Japan.
    REL060000 : RELIGION / Shintoism.
    POL034000 : POLITICAL SCIENCE / Peace.

There's a god

for that

for Hiroyuki and Tamae Yasunobu

The Japanese *kanji* on the front cover are the names of the tsunami-stricken cities of the Great Tōhoku Earthquake of 2011, in right-to-left reading order: Hachinohe, Kuji, Miyako, Yamada, Ōtsuchi, Kamaishi, Ōfunato, Rikuzentakata, Kesennuma, Minami-sanriku, Ishinomaki, Higashi-matsushima, Matsushima, Tagajō, Sendai, Natori, Iwanuma, Watari, Yamamoto, Soma, Minami-soma, Namie, Futaba, Tomioka, Naraha, Hirono.

CONTENTS

素 SIMPLICITY
 1 Celebrating 3
 2 Exploring 9
 3 Purifying 18
 4 Worshiping 25
 5 Disasters 30
 6 Connecting 36
 7 Evacuations 49
 8 Meditating 51
 9 Meltdowns 62
 10 Communing 65
 11 Floating 80
 12 Explosions 93
 13 Studying 95

混 COMPLEXITY
 14 Awaking 108
 15 Disappointments 114
 16 Worrying 117
 17 Giving 123
 18 Assessments 128
 19 Crying 131

禊 PURITY
 20 Ghosts of Tōhoku 144

Illustrations

Ōkuninushi-no-mikoto	xv
Sakaiminato	14
Matsue	20
Prefectures of Japan	32
Tōhoku	44
Izumo to Yunotsu	58
Tsuwano	82
Tectonics of Japan	88
Yunotsu to Hagi	94
Hagi	102
Hiroshima	132

Preface

Gentle readers,

In the days immediately following the Great Tōhoku Earthquake of 2011 many of you expressed concern for the safety of those you knew; I too received many heartfelt inquiries, which I responded to as best I could under the circumstances.

Upon my return from Japan, the unresolved crisis at the Fukushima nuclear power plant was still weighing heavily. Because of this, it was difficult to bring my recent journey through Japan to any sort of conclusion, and queries from those who care went unanswered. I did not yet know how to sort the jumble of my emotions.

In my lifetime I have learned that clarity of thought comes from the act of writing, and so, seeking clarity, I wrote. My story, a personal narrative of travels in Japan, is intertwined with the cataclysmic narrative that was occurring simultaneously: two very different scales juxtaposed, two very different measures of significance.

What follows is the interposition of these two stories: one played out on the international stage, whose outlines are presently well known to anyone who follows current events; the other a personal account of a journey through Japan at that same time.

There is also a third story, a tale of fantasy, as a concluding chapter, which you may find intriguing all by itself: it is a story that conveys my feelings for the future of this grief-stricken nation.

Joe Honton
July 2011. Sebastopol, California.

Acknowledgements

From inception to completion, it has been a blessing to receive encouragement and help from my muse, my first reader, my editor, my proofreader, my mother, Margaret Honton.

Special thanks also to my sister, Cathy Atwood, for being enthusiastic through it all.

PRONUNCIATION

The basics of the Japanese language can be mastered with a few rules: everything is phonetic, accentuation is subtle, there are five vowels. Here's some quick guidance to help you read nouns like a pro –

The alphabet contains 46 characters which are transliterated into the Latin alphabet using a pair of letters (a consonant and a vowel) so the sounds are written, ka, ki, ku, ke, ko . . . ma, mi, mu, me, mo . . . and so forth. When reading a new word for the first time, break the word into its consonant-vowel pairs and sound each of them out phonetically; this will provide you with passable pronunciation.

Japanese words don't often have strong accents, so pronounce each syllable with even stress.

There are five vowel sounds which are transliterated using a single letter of the English alphabet. But be careful here, because this is the key to the language. I pronounce the vowels as if they are comic book interjections: *Aah, Eee, Ooh, Eh, Oh*. Each of these is transliterated using a single letter: a, i, u, e, o.

/a/ sounds like *ahi tuna*
/i/ sounds like *enough*
/u/ sounds like *oodles*
/e/ sounds like *able*
/o/ sounds like *open*

The two confusing ones are /i/ which sounds like the English language long ē, and /e/ which sounds like the English language long ā. Some examples:

ayu is pronounced ă·yŭ

ikayaki is pronounced ē·kă·yă·kē

udon is pronounced ŭ·dōn

fue is pronounced fŭ·ā

onigiri is pronounced ō·nē·gē·rē

When a macron is placed above a vowel, it becomes a longer version of itself. This is often used with the /o/ sound, so the word Tōhoku would be pronounced Tō·ō·hō·kŭ.

Ōkuninushi-no-mikoto
Izumo-taisha

素

SIMPLICITY

1 章 CELEBRATING

Japan is a nation of festivals, and sooner or later, every visitor will stumble upon a city or town in the midst of celebration. Oh, what a delight to see the townsfolk honoring their local traditions, performing old rituals, fulfilling time-honored customs, enjoying themselves fully and without inhibition. I've often wondered, just what is it about Japanese festivals that makes them so compelling?

Japan's schedule of national holidays provides a rhythm to the calendar year that is unfamiliar to me. It's curious that New Year's Day, the first day of the first month, is the start of a sequence that continues with the third day of the third month, the Dolls' Festival, and the fifth day of the fifth month, Children's Day. But then the numerology stops, and the seventh day of the seventh month, which is Tanabata, the star festival, is passed over as a national holiday. Instead, the holiday calendar holds other surprises: Coming of Age Day, National Foundation Day, Spring Equinox, Showa Day, Constitution Day, Greenery Day, Ocean Day, Respect for the Aged Day, Autumn Equinox, Health and Sports Day, Culture Day, Labor Day, and the Emperor's Birthday. In all, sixteen national holidays: four of patriotism; four dedicated to children and elders; four celebrating nature; and four others given over to work, play, culture, and reflection. What other country celebrates family, nature, and culture with so many holidays?

3

Festivals are the local counterpart to the national holidays, providing hundreds of reasons to sing and dance and pray. Some festivals are directly related to the country's agrarian heritage: in mid-winter, prayers are made for the coming year's success; in spring, blessings upon the planting season are sought; in summer, appeals are made for protection from disease and drought; and in autumn, gratitude is offered for the bountiful harvest. Many of the festivals celebrate the enshrined *kami* by taking them out for a neighborhood stroll in a *mikoshi* – an elaborate palanquin suspended from bamboo poles, carried on the shoulders of the faithful. Thus the deity is paraded before the local townsfolk, bestowing its blessing and grace upon the passers-by.

The first Japanese *matsuri* that I encountered, many years ago, was one of the festivals dedicated to *Susanō-no-mikoto*, the god of the summer storm; I enjoyed this *Gion Matsuri* in Kokura, my wife's birthplace, during one of my many visits to Japan. During the festival, the enshrined god was ceremonially removed from the local Yasaka shrine, placed in a decorated *mikoshi*, and carried with great vigor and pride – over the course of three nights – through the local streets.

Susanō-no-mikoto is but one of the many gods that watch over Japan. Some say this country has a god for everything, and after a while you begin to agree.

Japan has a uniquely religious way of life, a life filled with the blessings of the gods – not one omnipotent creator, protector, benefactor, exemplar, adjudicator. Instead, Japanese *kami* take many forms: mythical gods that explain the order of the universe; place-based gods that inhabit mountains and groves and lakes and seas; ancient trees venerated as the earthly abode of heavenly visitors; mystic messengers in animal form; supernatural beings in the guise of ghosts and demons; martyrs and saints that become gods by example; and the spirits of ancestors who have long since crossed over. All these are *kami*, and all these imbue life with meaning and provide strength when called upon by the living.

That first *Gion Matsuri* had all the elements that most such religious festivals have: elaborate carriages, loud chants, athletic bearers, fervor and excitement. And the event was accompanied by strange and wonderful festival food, fireworks and sparklers, banners and flags, girls in pretty summer *yukata*. It was like a wild outdoor pajama party.

That festival was much like festivals everywhere, with an emphasis on food and friends and family (universal elements that cross cultural and national boundaries), but it differed in the participatory nature of the central event. *Matsuri* always seem to have some central physical activity – carried out by a team of strong bodies – one that somehow captivates the spectators, that is transmitted from the organized core to the by-standing chaos, that excites the crowd and induces an elevated state of mind. Somehow, the loud drumbeats, the chants, the rowdy shouts, all synchronize the very heartbeat of the crowd, so that the perspiration of the performers heightens the senses of the onlookers, magically inducing them to sway and sing and shout with spontaneous joy.

As a first-timer, I found it hard to recognize this as a religious event. Where were the pious leaders and their faithful followers? Where were the worshipful poses of the righteous? Where was the reverence and awe? None of these was present. It would take half a lifetime before I could drop my preconceived notions of sanctity, and allow myself to admit a different way, before I could see worship in the pure joy of abandon.

I've come to experience *matsuri* as worshipful events simply by recognizing their inside-out nature. My own Catholic upbringing taught me that communion with God was best carried out as an inner monologue; public exhortations/expostulations were best left to the "holy rollers" in their tents; and thankfulness for God's benevolence – no matter through what agency – was to be expressed with sincerity and gravitas, amen. *Matsuri* break from all of this, by turning everything inside out: inner monologue is replaced by joyful outbursts; shouts come not from the pulpit, but from the throng; and gratitude for bounty is not a tone-deaf chant but a feast and a celebration. The participants strip to the edge of impropriety, exposing their bodies as well as their souls, revealing their inner selves, leaving no room for the sanctimonious to hide.

Matsuri are singular events, a dramatic break from the daily routine, and they occur at the local level, here or there on different days. In contrast, the observance of *obon* occurs at a national level.

Of all the special days, I like *obon* the best. *Obon* is not a national holiday and it's not a festival in the same way that other *matsuri* are. *Obon* is much more personal: it is the annual observance of rituals, by families, in remembrance of their departed loved ones. The event occurs over a three-day period, beginning with the lighting of a small bonfire, *mukaebi*, in front of the family's *butsudan* to beckon the ancestral spirits to their former earthly home, and ending with another bonfire, *okuribi*, to release them back to the spirit world. Their passage is invoked, by visiting priests, with ritual and prayer. Once the spirits have returned to Earth, to their familial home, they join the living for a feast and a celebration.

Obon is a family time, and the days of observance are contemplative and reflective, as the living remember and honor the dead. Towards the end of the observance, the family expands to include friends and acquaintances, so that the nucleus becomes the community. And this inclusive community assembles in ways that look, outwardly, like the assemblies at other *matsuri*: lingering crowds, festive foods, drumming, singing, dancing. But there are differences between *obon* and other *matsuri*. With *obon*, the exuberance and abandon of the crowd are toned down to more respectful notes, the dancers tend to be more graceful, and the blessings bestowed resonate deeper.

Obon suits my temperament; its celebratory mood is at once pensive and solemn.

This year's *obon* weighs heavily upon the hearts of the people. This year, 2011, will be remembered for the great tragedies suffered by the country. The Japanese date 23年3月11日(金) – the twenty-third year of the *Heisei* era, third month, eleventh day – is stamped into the consciousness of the nation: an infamous day of tribulation. The celebratory mood of this year's *obon* is subdued by the memory of unfulfilled lives, abruptly ended; these days of communion with the dead, which are normally so joyous, are instead filled with sadness.

The story of this great tribulation was headlined by newspapers around the world as the magnitude of the earthquake shook our senses, as the toll of lives claimed by the tsunami was tabulated, as the meltdown at Fukushima brought us to the brink. Over and over, the news reports detailed the size of the destruction and number of deaths, and our senses grew numb to the facts and figures. The reports – without the essential details of lives, families, and communities – failed to convey the nation's true suffering. Even the compassionate outpouring globally during those first few days was overshadowed by other events.

This missing human story has left me in a state of sadness, in an unfinished place where lack of closure has set me searching for something – something whose contours are not yet fully defined . . . perhaps some way to understand what the survivors feel, some way to support them in their sadness without resorting to pity, some way to honor the dead for their individual contributions without referring to their collective numbers (as just a statistic), some way to look beyond the tragedy of Fukushima to a world that can wean itself of its dangerous nuclear habit.

I have tried to find the contours of this missing story by recounting my own tale of those days, with the hope that it may suggest other as-yet-unknown possibilities. So here is my tale: a tale of myths and *manga*, of castles and canals, of potters and painters, of pretty women and bus drivers, of spirits and ghosts, of gods and atomic bombs. Japan is a place I have come to love: its geography, its history, its language, its artistry, its scenery. And its underbelly: the rumbling earth, the grumbling politics, the flashing neon, and the go-go-go pace of life.

2 章 Exploring

I have lost count of how many times I've traveled to Japan, but it's probably a dozen over the course of three decades. In the early years, my attention was drawn to the novelty of pop culture and the surprises of a country that was more highly developed than my own. Later trips were more geared towards the growing family – my own children, our nieces and nephews – and the activities that young children enjoy. The early trips included visits to and activities in well-known places: Tokyo, Hiroshima and Nagasaki. We saw castles, gardens and quaint villages; mountains, waterfalls and volcanoes; fish markets, shopping districts and high-speed trains. But in the past decade I've had the opportunity to explore new regions that are off the beaten path: a visit to the tropical gardens of Okinawa; a second honeymoon to the hot springs of Yufuin; a solo journey through Kyushu and to the treasured island of Yakushima; and a tour of the mountain villages of Shirakawago, where families still roof their homes with grass thatch, in an architectural tradition that is four centuries old.

Now, once again, I find myself drawn to this endearing and oh-so-different land. What fresh discoveries await? Where will my explorations lead this time?

This year's trip is to be an exploration of Shimane and its surroundings. Our itinerary – my wife's and mine – is to travel down the coast, visiting Sakaiminato, Matsue, Izumo, Yunotsu,

Hamada, Tsuwano and Hagi before departing for Hiroko's hometown further south. Hiroko, my beloved, has been my tour guide, translator and companion for most of my earlier journeys in Japan; but of late, I have taken more initiative to plan and execute travel on my own. This trip is to have a mix of travel styles: some shared, some solo.

Shimane is situated on the southwest coast of Japan's main island of Honshu. With self-deprecating humor, Shimane promotes itself as the "47th most famous prefecture in Japan" (there are only 47 prefectures). It is remote and sparsely populated due to its geography. Mountains stand between Shimane to the north and the plains of Hiroshima to the south, making for difficult passage and accounting for its centuries of isolation. The mountains reach all the way to the sea, making a rugged coastline, one that is habitable only in a few choice spots. And these spots afford only a meager existence, for the soil is not naturally conducive to agriculture and the wind blows every day.

This is not the Japan we know. Here there are no gilded pagodas, no reflecting pools, no refined gardens. The pace of life is different too: shopping districts don't have those boisterous hucksters, buses aren't crammed with the weary-eyed, and trains wait at platforms just a little longer. This place is like a cabin in the woods compared to a mansion in the city, where the necessities of life are all that count. This is the other side of Japan.

The sea itself is the dominant force of Shimane; here the Kuroshio Current carries warm water up from the East China Sea through the Tsushima Strait on its way north to the Sea of Japan. The strait's strong flow increases as it squeezes between Korea and Japan, and the accompanying winds match this flow. Despite the fact that the current contains "warm" water, the inland effect is anything but warm, and the wind's constant presence drains a person's vital force. Only the rugged and the determined survive here. Indeed, this place was, for a long time, a final outpost, far from the court and politics of emperors and shoguns.

This day our journey brings us to the fishing and shipping port of Sakaiminato, where we immerse ourselves for a few hours in Japanese pop culture.

At the ferry/bus/train terminal I see signs in five languages: in Japanese, of course; in English, which is *de rigueur* for any tourist town; in Chinese, which in the past few trips I've seen in an increasing number of places; in Korean, which is to be expected since this is so close the Korean peninsula; and in Russian, which is a surprise to me (I have never before seen the Cyrillic alphabet in Japan).

I reflect on this intentional effort to become the gateway to Asia, and on this babel of languages. The Japanese have allowed the languages of its commercial partners and guests to slip into their culture, and evidence of this is everywhere.

I also reflect on the most notable exception to this trend: their native religion. This is one part of Japan where the language has not been tainted; religion still remains faithful to its mother tongue. And this fidelity is imperative, because the wisdom captured within the *kanji* names of people and places and events makes translation to a foreign language impossible. Too much hidden meaning is lost.

When Francis Xavier came to Japan in 1549 to teach Christianity, he toiled to understand the language of the people and to translate the teachings of the church, but his efforts were not a big success. He failed to understand the depth of the Japanese faith because he missed the hidden meaning of the language. The doctrine of original sin could not be explained to people who believed in the inherent goodness of the human soul. The threat of eternal damnation gained no traction for people who honored their ancestors . . . no, those souls were in a clean and bright place, and no salvation was needed.

Just as the Jesuits failed to understand the religion of this land, so too have countless others from the West failed. And how could they succeed? The religion has no founder whose life can be compared with Abraham or Jesus or Muhammad; it has no written scriptures whose doctrine can be challenged; it has no hierarchy whose power structure can be manipulated; it has no idols whose worship can be subverted.

The Japanese faith is theirs alone – influenced by Confucianism and Buddhism – but a truly indigenous religion, arising in antiquity from first principles, bound to the island nation, its people, its culture, its language. So the signs in five languages would be of no help in understanding the mysteries of this faith. I would have to learn to speak the language of the *kami*.

Sakaiminato is the birthplace of Mizuki Shigeru, the author of Japan's long-running, celebrated cartoon series, "Gegege-no-Kitaro". This *manga* tells the supernatural folkloric tales of grotesque and mischievous ogres and shape-shifters. Shigeru has been writing and drawing for more than five decades, and his work transcends its pop culture status the way the works of Charles Schultz and Walt Disney have transcended American pop culture, to become modern-day metaphysical parables.

Japanese folk tales are filled with ghosts and possessed animals, which upon first reading appear as familiar as the characters compiled by the Brothers Grimm, but which upon second reading seem to take shape as true spirits rather than allegorical stand-ins — ghosts wandering the waysides and invading candle-lit homes, desperately seeking release from their emotional shackles; mad women roaming the forests in vengeful pursuit of their wrongdoers; nocturnal animals appearing and disappearing, leaving messages from the other side. Shigeru extends this folk tradition, filling everything around us, even ordinary objects, with personality and spirit, but while his make-believe world is filled with the unexpected, it is always a playful world, where the frightful aspects of the spirits are only a reflection of the viewer's own fears, and where overcoming fear seems to be the tale's purpose.

Sakaiminato celebrates its "first citizen" with a museum dedicated to his life and work, and in a testament to their affection for him, the Japanese have opened the museum even before his life is complete. While the museum is enough to hold your interest for an hour or so, the walk *to* the museum is enough to captivate you for a day. The walk, from the train station to the museum, is along a straight, shop-lined street with an orderly assortment of vendors: stationary, hardware, handicrafts, fine art, snack stands and tea merchants; plus souvenir shops with shelves of *Gegege-no-Kitaro* ogre-emblazoned T-shirts, stuffed toys, coffee mugs, purses, and knick-knacks in the guise of useful household implements.

But the true delight of Mizuki Shigeru Road is its display of bronze statues depicting the author's creations. These artworks masterfully transform the flat creatures of the *manga* into fully

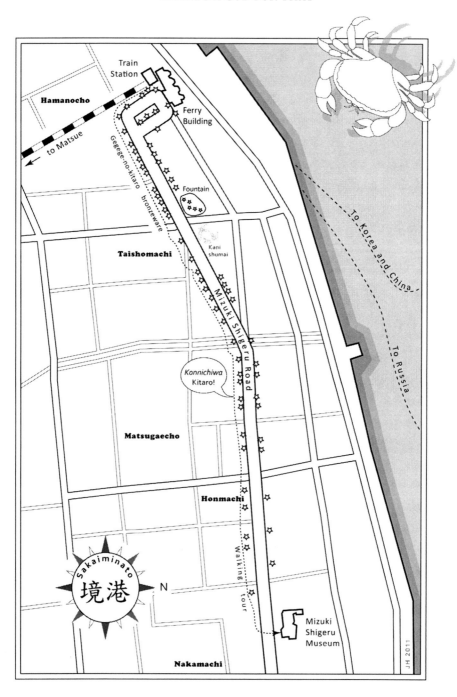

dimensioned *objets d'art*. Each is cast in bronze and mounted on granite. The statues are arranged singly or in groups of two or three, each depicting a demon-spirit or monster from Shigeru's repertoire. It was a delight to see Shigeru's tricksters, who inhabit the woods and waters of the wilds – foxes and fish and frogs and more. And it was a surprise to see the *inanimate* objects that he has somehow given a life and a personality – sticks, leaves, and dust-balls in the attic. And what a thrill to discover the artist's unexpected sense of proportion – each piece of art in its own scale, some life-sized, some exaggerated, some scaled down. Such variety imbues the bronze collection with a dynamic force that lifts them from their static representations into something much livelier and more compelling.

While walking down Mizuki Shigeru Road, delighting in the statues, we are startled to see Kitaro, the *manga's* namesake, approaching us in mascot form.

"Wow, great! Quick, get a picture!" Hiroko beams at me.

I quickly snap a couple of shots of Kitaro, dressed in his yellow-and-brown striped top.

He acknowledges us and waves, "*Konnichi-wa*", and then poses for the camera with his head cocked to one side and his palms flashing a sprightly "Hello".

Hiroko and I each get a quick hug from him, and off he goes.

"Lucky!" she exclaims.

Yes, this is like posing for snapshots with Snoopy at the Charles M. Schultz ice rink, or getting hugs from Mickey Mouse at Disneyland. We are as giddy as kids.

In Sakaiminato we encounter for the first time the strong winds of the Tsushima Strait, made even stronger by the town's location at the end of a sand spit: flanked by Lake Nakaumi to the west and Miho Bay to the east. The wind comes in spasms, catching us by surprise, blowing hats off, and making simple activities like opening a door a risky business. It is a messenger from the sea, sending us periodic reports in premonition of the latent energy – the strength and fury, just below the sea's surface – that is waiting to be released.

It is a *cold* wind, the kind that stings your cheeks, flushing your face, paradoxically warming your skin while chilling your core, and it purges our bodies, leaving us like empty vessels, ready to be filled with whatever comes our way. We are drained, and thus we are in a vulnerable state and our emptied bodies are susceptible to influences, both negative and positive. And with our bodies purged, our souls too are in an exposed position – we will have to be on guard.

While we are retreating from the museum back to the train station, the blue sky begins sending snow flurries that swirl violently with vortex and eddy. I search the sky for a "snow-bow," not remembering that the optics of raindrops and light is what causes a rainbow, and that snow can't produce such a show.

To escape the weather, we stop at a snack stand with a walk-up order window, purchase two crab-cake buns, and sit on an outdoor stoop under a canopy, hoping to refortify ourselves for the last segment of our walk. Crab is the local specialty. The guidebooks all recommend snow crab as an essential part of every visit to the town, and with good reason: almost two-thirds of the country's entire haul of snow crab comes through this port town. Packing plants are the town's principal industry. On our arrival at Yonago Airport last night, we ordered a serving of crab dumpling, which was both appetizing to look at – its white, red and rose-petal-pink contents visible through the translucent steamed wrapper – and tasty as well: firmly packed together, and with just a hint of salt, it set the standard for crab dumplings. But today's crab bun is a disappointment, not steamy fresh, but lacking all zest – and worst of all – its inner contents have an unappetizing brown-mustard color, without even a suggestion of pink. Ah well, even in a land of celebrated cuisine, there are disappointments.

In a final celebration of Shigeru's brand of culture, we board train cars painted inside and out with the brightly colored images of Shigeru's characters, and leave the port of Sakaiminato, heading inland to Matsue.

"Thanks for a great visit, Shigeru-san – *arigato!*"

3 章 Purifying

Matsue is the largest city in Shimane, and is the prefecture's capital, but with a population of only 190,000, it is tiny by Japanese standards. Here we were romanced by the city's water, its canals and castle, its wildlife, and its plentiful supply of regional cuisine.

The setting for the city accounts for much of its history: it is situated between Nakaumi and Shinjiko – two of Japan's largest lakes. Connecting the two is the Ohashi river.

Shinjiko is a fresh-water lake with just a hint of salinity, while Nakaumi, due to its tidal connection to the Sea of Japan, is more brackish. This diversity of fresh-water and salt-water leads to a diversity of wildlife, to the extent that the area is recognized by the Ramsar Convention as a "Wetland of International Importance." Water is the dominant force in Matsue.

The lakes and the river are naturally abundant in sea perch, shrimp and eel; the saturated plains to the east and west are wintering spots for migratory geese, ducks and swans, and shelter some two-hundred resident bird species. To the north and south the lakefront gently rises to forested mountains clothed with deciduous and evergreen species: oak, beech, pine, sweet-scented *Chamaecyparis*, and Japanese cedar.

With this abundant food supply and a ready source of building materials, the city of Matsue grew; moreover, its founders made good use of the flowing water. Canals were dug throughout the city, using water diverted from the Ohashi, and these canals served multiple needs: fresh water for daily use, a ready fire-fighting source, and a transportation network for commerce.

Matsue is a castle town, with the castle standing atop a small rise in the plain, affording an unbroken view of the lakes, the city, and the flats below. The canals completely encircle the castle, and for ten generations they have provided the first line of defense for the castle's occupants, the Matsudaira clan.

We visit the well-preserved castle and climb the broad cut-stone steps, up through three layers of defensive walls – proudly cut and assembled in 1607 – massive, free-standing split rock that still bears the stone-mason's hammered-in signature. I've always been fascinated by Japan's consummate skill in building walls that withstand the forces of rain and frost and gravity. My own pitiful attempts to hold earth in place (garden walls, retaining walls, etc.) have taught me to respect Japanese stone masons. I especially like the way the walls gracefully curve inward and upward, in imitation of a tree trunk that grows out of the earth: it reminds me of the *kanji* character for people 人, two simple strokes, one resting on the other, neither able to stand on its own.

Today, the Matsue canals are plied by shallow-draft boats which provide tourists with a romantic view of the old town and castle. These long, narrow boats are designed for comfort, Japanese style: they provide floor seating on either side of a blanket-draped *kotatsu* (that curious low table with the hidden heating element that is found in every Japanese home).

We board one of these boats, so inviting, so romantic, because we are on holiday and feel inclined to romance. Overhead, a canopy is stretched over an aluminum skeleton, thus keeping passengers dry on rainy days and cool on sunny days. The sun

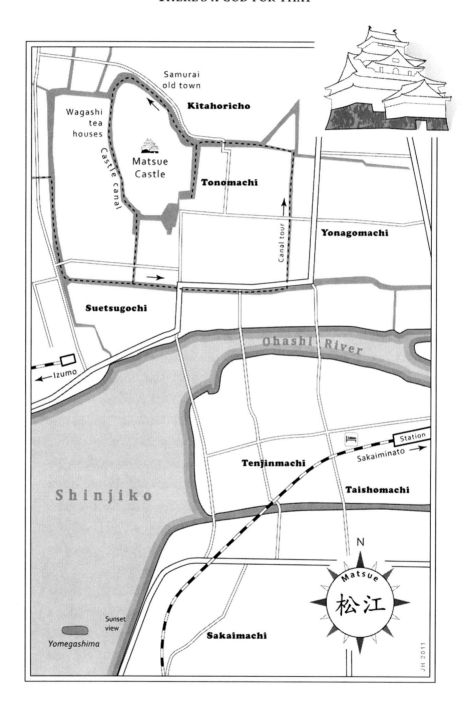

struggles to break through the low overcast that just this morning was sending flurries of soft pellets down upon us. Fortunately, the *kotatsu's* comforter and the overhead canopy are a perfect defense against the weather. This being only the 10th of March, there are few tourists, and the two of us share the boat with only one other passenger and the boatman.

Our tour circuits the castle, passing the authentic samurai homes of the old town; countless numbers of picturesque bridges; the city's new museum (set for its grand opening within the week); and portions of the city's administrative complex. Throughout the ride, the castle's strong presence is felt, even when obscured from direct view.

The area's diverse wildlife has accommodated itself to the canal. We have approached a great blue heron and other endemic waterfowl, some a novelty to me, startling none by our presence; they keep to their perches, with unruffled feathers.

As we near the final turn and the end of the tour, the boatman sings his rendition of the Matsue Song, a lyrical folk tune celebrating the abundance of gifts that this water city has given its citizens. I don't understand many of the words that he is crooning, yet allow myself to be carried along by the sentimental tale.

The waters that surround and flow through Matsue (Lake Nakaumi, Lake Shinjiko, the Ohashi, and the canals) provide something more than just a romantic setting. They also provide a purifying medium. In traditional Japanese religious practice, water is the primary medium for *misogi*, a rite of purification. This rite is observed by visitors at every shrine, when they dip a bamboo ladle into the fountain of fresh water located just inside the shrine's inner gate, to wash their hands and rinse their mouth before worship. For believers, this symbolic act, especially when performed with a pure heart, washes away worldly troubles, and readies their souls to receive the grace of the gods.

Originally *misogi* was performed as an elaborate ritual at the shoreline of flowing rivers, preferably ones that were close to the sea. There, the unclean thoughts that were released would be carried downstream, and the sea's salt would intensify the cleansing. Matsue – with the Ohashi's strong current and Lake Nakaumi's saline water – is an ideal place for this type of *misogi*.

We do not follow that elaborate ritual of ablutions and baths today, but still I like to think that we are receiving some special grace from the waters of the canal, which course through the city, purifying everything and everyone in its path.

A species of clam native to the Ohashi – and measuring just ½ inch across – has been harvested and consumed by the townsfolk since its founding. We enjoy this repast at our morning meals, prepared in a light soup.

These morning meals, served buffet style in the hotel lobby, are spread before us with an overabundance of both Western and Japanese choices. Our first breakfast here leaves us bewildered by the choices; Hiroko and I each take samples as if it were a pot-luck party, each of us with a different assortment on our plates. We taste this and that, remarking in low voices about each local specialty, careful not to disturb the other guests who share our common table. As we near the end – our plates now reduced to a few choice items, carefully kept with expectation that the last morsel would leave our palates fresh – I have on my plate two plump, red *umeboshi*. Knowing how much Hiroko enjoys these, and seeing that she has none, I use my chopsticks to delicately transfer one of my precious gems to her rice bowl. (Now, as I write, I must admit that my gesture was not completely unselfconscious, because I placed it artfully, perfectly imitating the grace and simplicity of Hiroko's culture, and noting with satisfaction that the red plum on the white rice formed a perfect image of the national flag.) My action, carried out with the affection of twenty-nine years of marriage, is spontaneous, an intimate moment, a private playful morning joke. But the gesture is caught by the woman on the opposite side of our table, who smiles at having witnessed this endearing act, and who cannot refrain from quiet laughter as she tries to explain to her companion what she has just seen. If I was at all inclined to embarrassment, I should have been blushing. But I too was delighted to have stumbled upon someone who liked my joke. It was a flirtatious moment between that stranger and me, carried out completely without words.

Matsue's culinary treat is *wagashi*, the bite-sized, wholly Japanese confection made of fresh pounded rice and filled with sweet bean paste. In Matsue, the handmade *wagashi* are presented in artful colors with a delightful variety of accents: fruity strawberry, buttery chestnut, minty *shiso*. We enjoy ours served with traditional green tea at a four-seated patisserie overlooking the canal and the castle. We are served, by not one, but three, effusive young girls who have an "Oh my, I'm actually serving a foreigner!" demeanor.

Late that afternoon we board the last city bus to make its rounds, which at this time of day extends its normal route, taking visitors to the eastern shore of Shinjiko where the sun sinking into the lake provides a panorama for photographers. The bus arrives at the opportune time, and we join the gathering crowd of amateur photographers paying nightly homage to the sun. On cue, the sun descends into the waters of Shinjiko, painting the sky with romance. Just offshore, Yomegashima's wind-gnarled pines lose their evergreen; transformed into dark silhouettes, they become the stuff of imagination.

Legend tells us that the island of Yomegashima first formed not too many years ago. As it rose up from the waters of Shinjiko – all in one night – it carried the body of a young woman who, just the day before, had gone missing from her abusive husband. The townsfolk, to honor her pious life, buried her body on the island, and dedicated the place to *Benzaiten,* the goddess of the sea, and erected *komainu* and *torii* (a pair of stone lions and a gate), facing the mainland, to protect the shrine.

Today, the *komainu* and *torii* are visible throughout the twilight hour, creating for us a contemplative mood, allowing us to reflect on the impermanence of life. And in the fleeting moments before darkness descends, we give thanks for all that we have received.

We are blessed this day, and we know it.

4 章 WORSHIPING

Hiroko and I depart from the water city, making our way to separate destinations: she advances to the village of Yunotsu to begin her study of the performing art, *Iwami-kagura*, and I lag behind for a pilgrimage to nearby Izumo-taisha, one of Japan's designated national treasures.

Just as Matsue is the political capital of Shimane, Izumo is the spiritual capital of Shimane. Mythologically, this remote outpost is considered to be the birthplace of Japan. And, according to the myths, once a year Shimane also becomes the place of the gods. Elsewhere in Japan the month of October is known as *kannazuki*, "the month of no gods," but here in Shimane, October is known as *kamiarizuki*, "the month when the gods are present," because, as Shinto myths assert, this is where eight million deities congregate for the month. Myths are foreign to me and I don't understand how others interpret meaning from them, but I am curious and willing to learn, so I await what revelations may come.

Izumo-taisha is old. The Kojiki ("Records of Ancient Matters"), dating to the year 712, tell the story of the sun goddess *Amaterasu-ōmikami* presenting Izumo-taisha to *Ōkuninushi-no-mikoto*, the god of fortune and the celestial matchmaker. Exactly when this was supposed to have occurred is not recorded, but by the year 950, there is a description of the shrine as being the highest building in the kingdom, perched on tall pillars, with a stairway to heaven ascending 48 meters. Around the year 1200,

25

the shrine was rebuilt to a more modest, and presumably a more maintainable, height. The most recent reconstruction of the shrine occurred in 1744; this is the building that stands today.

Bachelors and maidens come here seeking help in finding their soul mate, while young couples come here to bless their union. This is the sacred place where the eight million deities assemble each October to discuss the upcoming year's births, deaths and marriages.

There are many shrines in Japan. The Engi Shiki ("Detailed Laws of the Engi Period") written in the year 927, lists 2,861 shrines by name; today the number is estimated to be close to 87,000. Shrines are of various size, some consisting simply of a sacred rock or tree, protected only with a rope. Others, like Izumo, achieve the status of *taisha*, or grand shrine. Originally shines had no buildings, they were simply places where the gods descended from the heavenly realm. This type of shrine was cared for by the community – kept clear of overgrowth, swept clean of fallen leaves, and regularly freshened with offerings from worshipers. Later, shrines evolved to incorporate all of the basic elements we see today: an enclosing fence to delineate the sacred space; a *torii* to welcome worshipers; a *shimenawa* (rope of twisted, rice grass) to ward off unclean spirits; and a fountain of water for use in *misogi* purification. The Japanese word for shrine, *yashiro*, suggests an original meaning of "temporary structure", thus, shrines were thought of as power spots where the *kami* could be invoked. Over time, permanent facilities were added to shrines and special buildings for worshipers, priests, offerings, and sacred dances were added, and at these shrines the *kami* are thought to have taken up permanent residence. Today there is a range of shrines from simple to elaborate, but I like the simple ones: when they have been well tended, and the grounds have been swept clean, and the morning dew is still fresh on the paths, I can feel the presence of the *kami*, and I know that the rest of my day will be good.

While making plans for the next incarnation of Izumo's main worship hall, archaeologists excavating in 2000 unearthed the preserved remains of one of the original 13th century pillars: three massive cedars bound together to form a single column! These remains are now housed nearby in a new museum, so after finishing my walking tour of the shrine's grand promenade and outer grounds, I go to the Museum of Ancient Izumo.

The museum's contents and its superb galleries and exhibits are impressive. The highlights for me are the bronze bells, swords, and artifacts, some of them dating to the third century. There is a photograph of one of these ancient bronze bells featured on the museum's brochure, so I pay special attention. The bronze had that nearly uniform green patina that all aged bronze becomes; the metal was thin, like wrought sheet metal (not thick or cast from a molten pour); the construction was of three assembled pieces – one semi-circular top-piece, and two bottom halves that were somehow joined, along well-defined seams, into a fluted shape, with the bottom opening flaring out to become slightly wider than the closed crown. The wrought metal was stamped with simple straight-lined patterns (neither intricate, nor resembling any symbolic patterns that I have seen elsewhere). This was a bell designed to be struck with a hand-held hammer or stick; it had no interior clapper. Just what the bell was used for, I can only guess, but probably something ceremonial. This was an object whose cultural place in Japan's history pointed to as-yet-unknown realms. The mystery of this artifact's maker, and his predecessors and his successors, captivates me. I allow my thoughts to wander over the possibilities, wondering at the simple and the profound, transfixed in my gaze.

Here is a side of Japan I have never before encountered. I linger in each gallery, studying the patterns and forms, and delighting in these treasures. I am surprised when the PA system announces closing time, before I have the chance to see the final two galleries. I am the last one out, just as two remaining cars desert the museum's parking lot.

I arrive at the designated 6 p.m. serving time, in the hostel's common room, for my dinner. The hostess is prompt, bringing all the customary and expected dishes: tea, rice, *miso* soup, broiled fish, mountain vegetables and fresh fruit; what I've come to call the "roots and shoots" dinner. This type of dinner is always served with a multitude of special-purpose crockery: a round wooden bowl for the soup, a funnel-shaped bowl for rice, rectangular plates matched in proportion to the fish of the day, two-inch square bowls for prepared vegetables, three-inch round bowls for fruit, and a cook's assortment of thumb-sized ceramics and pinch-pots for single-serve dumplings, spiced condiments, pickles or seaweed garnishes. The presentation of the meal is an important part of the dinner ritual, and an examination of the bowls and plates is a sure-fire conversation starter, as are remarks about the chef's choice of local food. Gathered vegetables, in particular, have a great degree of variety: some coming from the sea – *arame, konbu, wakame, hijiki, mozuku, nori*; some from the mountains – *warabi, mitsuba, fukinotō, take*; some from secret family gathering spots – *matsutake*. And cultivated vegetables add to the variety: three-foot long *gobō*; nine-holed *renkon* that looks like a cartwheel when sliced; slippery/slimy *satoimo*; and the ubiquitous *daikon*. I enjoy my "roots and shoots," and appreciate the predominance of underground and wild-crafted vegetables, which are never served in unadorned heaps, the way corn, peas and carrots often are back in Sebastopol.

Following customary protocol, the television is turned on by the hostess with a click of the remote control. I am the only guest this night, so when she retreats to the kitchen I am left to myself.

And now I see images of a cataclysm. . . .

5 章 DISASTERS

FRI MAR 11, 2011 2:46 PM JST. SENDAI, MIYAGI PREF. Latent energy has been accumulating in the Japan Trench east of Sendai since 1933, in geologic time a scant 78 years. This latent energy is suddenly released as the North American plate, to the west, snaps upward along a 300-kilometer long underwater fault line, allowing the adjacent Pacific plate, to the east, to slip below its crust. Tectonic movement is first detected by seismometers at 14:45 JST, triggering an early warning system that alerts citizens to an impending earthquake. Approximately one minute later, Japan's largest and most populous island of Honshu begins shaking.

During the next several minutes, the torn fissure at the epicenter cascades into a series of ruptures rippling north and south along its fault line, situated under the Pacific Ocean, 130 kilometers east of the city of Sendai. The earth's mantle grinds laterally over itself, east and west, as much as twenty meters, along the zone of subduction; vertical thrust is estimated to be as much as 30-40 meters.

A ten-centimeter drop in ocean-wave height is instantaneously measured at the nearest coastal station in Kamaishi. Two minutes later a ten-centimeter rise in ocean wave height is measured at Ishinomaki, one hundred kilometers to the south. Like a bathtub that is disturbed by a fallen object, these instantaneous changes in surface elevation, measured far away along the rim, are only a precursor to what is set in motion, ripples on sea skin, a faint clue to the massive sub-surface displacement that has begun its journey. The Japan Meteorological Agency, detecting the jolt, with the aid of a computer model, determines that a major tsunami of up to three meters in Iwate and Fukushima prefectures, and of up to six meters in Miyagi prefecture, is likely to occur as a result of the upheaval. It broadcasts an official tsunami warning to residents along the Tōhoku Coast.

FRI MAR 11, 2:46 PM. TOKYO. Seismic monitors detect the impending earthquake, triggering an automatic shutdown of Japan Railway's bullet trains. The railway's 27 high-speed trains quickly brake to a safe stop about fifteen seconds *before* the earthquake begins. Hundreds of regional and local trains and subways are notified by other means that an earthquake is happening and engineers stop all trains in their tracks. All platform departures are suspended.

Eleven nuclear reactors at Onagawa, Fukushima and Tokai begin automatic shutdown, as part of their standard operating protocol, in response to the onset of the earthquake.

Television and radio broadcasts are interrupted by the emergency public broadcast system, which announces the presently occurring earthquake's intensity and geographic distribution. Drivers are instructed to use caution, while building occupants are advised to seek safety immediately.

An orderly first response in an orderly country.

FRI MAR 11, 2:54 PM. KESENNUMA, MIYAGI PREF. An offshore GPS buoy east of Kesennuma is the first instrument to detect the approaching tsunami. It measures six meters in height. The Japan Meteorological Agency updates its tsunami warning for the

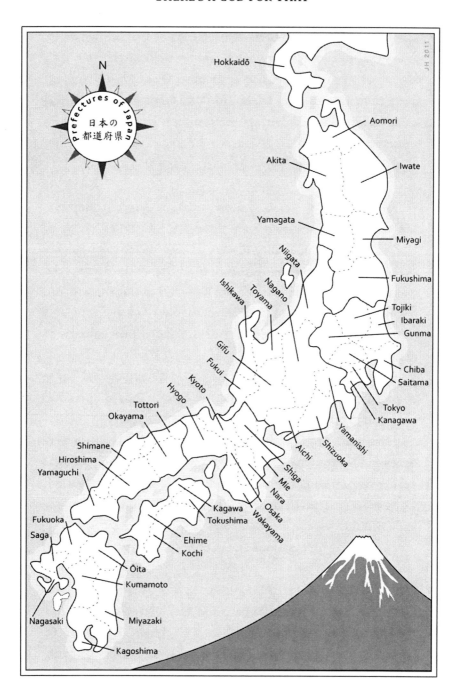

N

Prefectures of Japan

日本の
都道府県

Hokkaidō

Aomori

Akita

Iwate

Yamagata

Miyagi

Niigata

Fukushima

Nagano

Ishikawa

Toyama

Tojiki

Ibaraki

Gunma

Gifu

Fukui

Chiba

Saitama

Kyoto

Hyogo

Tottori

Okayama

Tokyo

Kanagawa

Yamanishi

Shizuoka

Shimane

Aichi

Hiroshima

Shiga

Yamaguchi

Mie

Nara

Kagawa

Osaka

Tokushima

Wakayama

Fukuoka

Ehime

Saga

Kochi

Ōita

Kumamoto

Nagasaki

Miyazaki

Kagoshima

Tōhoku Coast, first issued at 2:49 p.m., revising the impending wave's expected height upwards, to as high as ten meters.

FRI MAR 11, 3:15 PM. ŌFUNATO, IWATE PREF. The tsunami comes ashore at this fishing port of 42,000 people. It is measured at 3.2 meters in height, but – due to the funnel shape of Ōfunato's bay and the amplifying effect of the shallow ocean floor – the wave reaches a shoreline elevation of 23.6 meters.

[In the subsequent weeks, Ōfunato officials count 3629 houses destroyed or partially destroyed and 321 people killed by the wave; in addition, 140 others remain unaccounted for and are presumed to have been washed out to sea.]

Over the next several minutes, from 3:15 to 3:21, the tsunami arrives up and down the Tōhoku coastline, alternately crashing into remote rocky headlands, or funneling-amplifying into populated village-lined bays. Up and down the Tōhoku coast, twenty cities each confirm casualties in excess of one hundred.

Hardest hit is Miyagi prefecture: Iwanuma (178), Tagajō (186), Watari (251), Onagawa (473), Minami-sanriku (514), Sendai (683), Natori (901), Kesennuma (930), Higashi-matsushima (1031), Ishinomaki (2964).

To the north, in Iwate prefecture: Ōfunato (321), Miyako (412), Yamada (566), Ōtsuchi (765), Kamaishi (837), Rikuzentakata (1490).

To the south, in Fukushima prefecture: Iwaki (303), Soma (424), Minami-soma (504).

Twenty-three other cities as far north as Aomori and Hokkaidō prefectures, and as far south as Ibaraki and Chiba prefectures, count casualties, though less than one hundred each.

Just as in Ōfunato, the wave totally destroys buildings, boats, ports and infrastructure.

In addition to the confirmed death of 15,000 people, there are 8,000 people swept out to sea.

FRI MAR 11, 3:41 PM. FUKUSHIMA POWER PLANTS. The tsunami arrives at the Fukushima Daiichi and Fukushima Daini power plants, at heights of 10 and 12 meters, surging over the seawalls specifically built to protect the facilities from such surges. The seawater fills the basements of the reactor buildings at Fukushima Daiichi, where emergency diesel generators are housed. The diesel generators are designed to be used as part of the facility's fail-safe system, which includes electricity generated by the power plant itself, plus electricity from its connection to the outside grid, plus power from the reactor's steam-driven cooling system.

Three of Daiichi's six nuclear reactors are in hot shutdown mode when the tsunami arrives, with fuel rods having been automatically removed fifty-five minutes before, when sensors detected the impending earthquake. With the earthquake itself having damaged the region's electricity grid, and with a general power blackout throughout much of eastern Japan, the power plants are, ironically, out of power. The diesel generators at the site, which have been running during the hour between the earthquake and the tsunami, are rendered inoperable once they have been submerged in seawater.

With the fail-safe generators no longer usable, batteries are placed in service. With the batteries connected, cooling water is circulated through the two largest reactors that are in hot shutdown: units 2 and 3. But engineers are unable to make this work for the smaller unit 1. The lifespan of the batteries is limited, and desperate calls are made for replacements. No follow-up to this is recorded.

The batteries are exhausted eleven hours later and the plant is without any means to pump its all-important cooling water through the reactors.

6 章 CONNECTING

As I sit in the hostel's common room, alone, my dinner getting cold, my attention fixed on the television, I try to assess the situation and wonder what my response should be.

The Japanese are no strangers to earthquakes. Big ones or little ones. They have grown up with regular drills. They have lived through collapse and fire and loss of life repeatedly. They have re-engineered, re-architected, redesigned, and rebuilt their homes and workplaces and shops and infrastructure to make the inevitable safe and survivable. And to a very large extent they have succeeded.

I am no stranger to the earth's rumblings, either. My first night in Japan, thirty years ago, was my initiation rite. When I was rocked out of bed, I called out one of the few Japanese words I knew: *jishin.* "Was that an earthquake?" my one-word question was asking. On another trip, a few years later, I saw a boarded-up Narita Airport where hundreds of large panes of glass had shattered from an earthquake just two days prior. And in Kyushu, the "Ring of Fire" proved its namesake true when, shortly after my departure, Mt. Aso erupted, yet again, producing ash and flow that buried the town I had been staying in.

So my reaction to what I am seeing on the television isn't immediate or decisive; it is studied and analytical: when did it happen, how intense was it, which cities are affected? The answer to "when" is easy to pick out from the announcer's steady stream:

2:46 p.m. (which means that it happened while I was transfixed by the ancient bronze bells of Izumo). The answer to "how intense" is now on the screen: 8.9 on the Richter scale – an alarming number [later revised to 9.0]. But the answer to "which cities" is not obvious because, while the television shows a map with the epicenter's location far from land, another on-screen map is blinking red and yellow all along the country's eastern coast. I have no one to help me translate the legend or what those blinking coastlines are meant to communicate.

I make a hurried telephone call to Hiroko, who is in the seaside village of Yunotsu, about forty kilometers away. Like everyone else in the country, my initial reaction is to check on the safety of those I know, which this time I limit to one person. But for most people in Japan, this means a whole network of family, friends, and associates.

I do not know exactly how the residents of Tokyo are reacting at this time, but I can imagine, based on my own experience in San Francisco of the moments immediately after the Loma Prieta earthquake of 1989. The memories of that time, two decades ago – of the need to connect, of the uneasy feelings caused by rumors, and of the surreal nature of what was happening – are still vivid in my mind.

During that earthquake, telephone traffic increased hour by hour as news from the region made its way across the country and into the late-night news hours of Eastern, Central and Mountain time zones; before making its way around the globe and into the morning news of, first Asia, and then Europe. People needed to connect. As incoming phone calls began to flood the switches, more and more people began to get busy signals; this in turn, only caused more traffic, as phone numbers were redialed repeatedly, in fruitless efforts to get through. By the time Europe woke up, no one could place a call to San Francisco, and exaggerated rumors of the city falling into the Pacific began to sound plausible. The regional phone company, Pacific Bell, in an effort to help first responders, decided to choke all incoming traffic and to give priority to phone calls originating from the affected areas. People could call out, but not in.

Loma Prieta struck at 5:04 p.m. The minutes and hours that followed still remain fresh in my mind. I never made it home that night.

After the shaking stopped, I hurried to get on the Bay Bridge, my mind projecting wild thoughts for my family's safety, for my home's integrity, and about the chaos that was surely awaiting me on the other side of the Bay. But getting on the Bay Bridge was an unfortunate choice. Traffic immediately came to a complete standstill. With no forward movement, we all got out of our cars for a first-hand view, looking backward at the city, now eerily quiet; and straining forward across the Bay, to our homes and communities. Were the first radio reports of the disaster's reach true?

As we stood on the bridge, scanning the skylines of the cities for signs that would tell us what was happening, a rumor began to travel, that the tunnel on Yerba Buena Island had collapsed. Another rumor soon followed, instructing us to turn our vehicles around and head back to San Francisco. Moments later we received word that, no, the tunnel hasn't collapsed. We turned our cars around again, and felt comical at our own expense, but at least we were doing something.

Rumors began to firm into facts: a segment of the bridge, on the other side of Yerba Buena, had broken, cars had fallen into the water, our way home was impassible, and we would have to wait our turn to evacuate.

Much later, when I finally arrived at Yerba Buena, I decided to follow my first instinct: to connect. I wanted to place that all-important call to Hiroko to tell her I was okay and to make sure that she was out of danger. And when I got my chance at the one phone on the island I kept it short, out of courtesy to the others waiting in the long line. "I'm okay. I won't be home tonight. I'll see you tomorrow."

This need to connect is universal: as I *needed* to connect when I was waiting my turn on the Bay Bridge; I *need* to connect now, when I find myself alone at the Izumo youth hostel. The entire population of Tokyo *needs* to connect now as it finds itself without electricity and without a way home; most of Japan, and even much of the world, *needs* to connect to assure themselves that their loved ones are safe.

Yet beyond the basic need to connect, is another more psychic need, which came to me as I retraced my route back to San Francisco after making that telephone call. *It was the need to make the event real.* While the earth was shaking, while construction cranes swung untethered high above, and while brick façades were crumbling, crashing onto parked cars, setting off alarms – those fascinating moments were real. But, strangely, listening for news on the radio, searching the skyline for signs, waiting on that bridge, was not real – because it felt like nothing was happening. That sensibility all changed the very instant that I finally connected. The simple act of voicing what had happened, made it real and caused me to tremble again, as reality set in.

As I began my retreat to San Francisco the charcoal sky advanced to meet the darkness of night; the bridge was eerily empty, only stragglers remained, walking in ones and twos; the choppy sea sent spasms of chilled air across the decks; fires in the distance glowed red, silhouetting the darkened cityscape. Reality was lonely, dark and cold.

And now, with Loma Prieta on my mind, I watch the television and see the confused actions of people in Tokyo: seeking information, reacting to rumors, and placing telephone calls. I am moved to tears as I see them receiving emergency kits with space blankets, bottled water, and ready-made meals. This is their moment of acceptance – yes, this is really happening. And what of all those people who depend upon trains to get them home, beginning their long walk into the darkness – will they make it?

But now, as then, I am also relieved, being able to connect with Hiroko. As time ticks away from the epicenter, brief exchanges will be repeated by others and news will reach friends and then friends of friends, until millions of people will know the situation in Japan. Just as I have called from Izumo to Yunotsu, Hiroko calls from Yunotsu to Kokura to learn that her parents are both safe; our son Luke calls from California to Kokura, indirectly learning that we are safe; my mother in Colorado calls California, and is relieved to hear Luke say, "Yes, they are safe." Then my relatives in Florida, North Carolina, Oregon, Ohio and Massachusetts, receive an email from Colorado: "I've heard that they are safe." Connections made, information exchanged, networks in action.

The network, for the most part, works, although perhaps not to the satisfaction of all; in this age of instant global communications we've come to expect everything to "just work" all the time. In Tokyo and elsewhere in Japan, people were able to connect in those first few critical hours. But along the eastern coast of Japan, with power knocked out, and with branch switches rendered inoperable from direct and indirect damage, there was no possibility of connecting. The lack of connection triggered the worst of fears, and as it turned out, rightly so. The script played out much as it did in the aftermath of Loma Prieta: people tried and tried again, switches became more and more overloaded, and busy signals became the norm. Cellphones only exacerbated the problem. With such a powerful tool at hand, millions of people began using their phones as private news devices, checking Internet sources for bulletins to find out what was happening elsewhere. Predictably, the phone system had to be reined in, and authorities issued pleas to restrict usage to emergency needs.

With my dinner still spread before me, I succumbed to the apprehensions of what I was witnessing, and in that state of distress my appetite disappeared, a natural reaction for sure. But for those who don't know of the Japanese fondness for food, I must say: for the Japanese, food is more than just a meal, more than just a way to take in calories. Food, with all its ancillaries – farming, fishing, harvesting, pickling, preserving, cooking, arranging, serving – takes top place in Japanese culture, surpassing the role of sex in our own culture. In Japan, advertising features food the way Madison Avenue features sex. Food sells. Finding good food is an ongoing pilgrimage, and – good or bad – whatever is served is always eaten. But here in this moment of unfolding crisis, with my stomach reacting to what I am witnessing, I abandon my unfinished meal, apologize to the hostess for the transgression, and return to my bunk room to watch the television coverage in private.

I watch the news for the next four hours, until the hostel's official "lights out" curfew hour of 10 o'clock.

Grasping at the announcer's meaning, I retrieve my pocket-sized Yohan dictionary and search for unfamiliar vocabulary: damage, destruction, injuries, casualties – words that my compact traveler's companion was not designed for. Some of the stronger words I can guess from context or familiarity: closures, explosions, deaths; while the dual tragedy's key words – *jishin* and *tsunami* – need no translation.

More frustrating, though is my unfamiliarity with the *kanji* of basic place-name geography: Aomori 青森 Iwate 岩手 Miyagi 宮城 Fukushima 福島 Ibaraki 茨城 Chiba 千葉. These, the east coast prefectures, stretching for 425 kilometers, are blinking red and yellow on the map in the lower corner of the television screen, communicating – without the need for names – the scale and extent of the event.

These are the communities in crisis, the announcer reading from fresh reports as they arrive in random order, snippets of information, an unbroken sequence, a roll call of disaster:

Hachinohe,

Kuji,

Miyako,

Yamada,

Ōtsuchi,

Kamaishi,

Ōfunato,

Rikuzentakata,

Kesennuma,

Minami-sanriku,
Ishinomaki,
Higashi-matsushima,
Matsushima,
Tagajō,
Sendai,
Natori,
Iwanuma,
Watari,
Yamamoto,
Soma,
Minami-soma,
Namie,
Futaba,
Tomioka,
Naraha,
Hirono.

These are coastal cities where time reveals and videos record, second-by-second, not just a wave, not a crest, but an unstoppable mass that lunges and churns from sea to earth, that heaves and swirls over seawalls, that crushes and swallows lives and hope.

One report after another is handed to the announcer, pressed into duty by the urgency of stranded commuters, the needs of information-starved officials, and the watchful nation of citizens that just need to know. The announcer, in short-sleeved shirt and without a tie, is clearly not the polished anchor of the nightly news, but he serves well. And the production team makes do as well: stitching together video clips as they come in, cutting in with hastily called briefings from first-response leaders, dispatch-

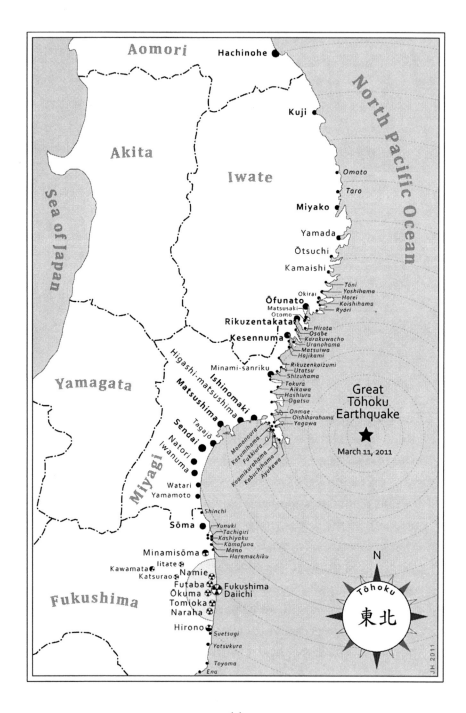

ing reporters and camera crews to Tokyo's transportation hubs, composing one bulletin after another for the announcer to read. These first bulletins are weighted toward the status of Tokyo: its train service, any open roads, the extent of the blackout (especially as night approaches), where people are finding food (since most eateries are without electricity, thus closed). And throughout the announcer's staccato of news, he himself is overridden by the emergency public broadcast system announcing aftershocks as they occur.

Then "man on the street" interviews begin to be filed, as NHK crews manage to get communications established with their studio command center. One reporter has encamped at Shinjuku Station, where, over the next several hours, he files reports on the status of the Yamanote Line (Tokyo's inner loop that serves millions of riders each day) and JR East's suburban lines. Another reporter calls in from Lawson's and AM-PM convenience stores, where shelves were emptied of batteries, cup-a-noodles, and bottled drinks within the first couple of hours. Another has filed reports from outside a major hub – was it Shibuya or Hamamatsucho or Akihabara? it could have been any of them (and probably was all of them) – showing a taxi stand with no taxis and a bus terminal with empty bays, and thousands of commuters waiting in lines that snaked around the block. Another has filed reports on the complete gridlock that occurred on the roadways, both major and minor, as movement in any direction was blocked when everyone simultaneously attempted to exit Tokyo's commercial, government and business districts. Then as daylight faded, and the stranded sized up their options, sales clerks and white-collar salary-men began walking, with or without flashlights, to their suburban homes an unknown number of hours away. Those who weren't fit enough for such an adventure began their long wait in public spaces, on chairs, on the floor, or in opened rail cars. In some places, first-response coordinators handed out small emergency care boxes containing water and snack food and blankets.

While Tokyo coped with all the inconveniences that the power outage brought, news from the Tōhoku Coast began to arrive. The first early helicopter shots of the tsunami were broadcast, shifting our attention away from Tokyo (which was merely inconvenienced) and towards the unfolding horror of the tsunami.

One of these video clips has haunted me ever since: a helicopter, following the tsunami's track in a high-level panorama, vividly captured the churning mass and its crushing force as it swallowed telephone poles and outbuildings, as it raced across level ground, before reaching an embankment that was four or five meters in height above the farmland. Atop this embankment, two cars were racing to safety. The drivers, seeing that they would be overtaken no matter how fast they might go across the levee, sharply turned off the embankment, down a farm road that crossed it at ninety degrees, and followed a new course of escape that put the oncoming tsunami directly behind them instead of broadside to their movement. At least one of the cars was able to outpace the tsunami. But the other car appeared to be within seconds of being overrun. As this high-speed drama was unfolding, the helicopter was gaining altitude and the cameraman was shifting his camera's view-port to gain a wider perspective of the whole tsunami; thus, the pilot and cameraman were oblivious to the human drama in the corner of their screen. And just seconds before the car made its escape – or didn't – the drama was lost off the edge of the screen. That driver has been on my mind ever since. Did she outpace the wave, or did it pick her up like a surfboard and carry her forward? Did she suffer injuries or was she a fatality? If she somehow made it to safety, what of her loved ones, her neighbors, her home, her livelihood? And how would she cope with having survived?

That haunting image, for me, tipped the balance of the day's events away from the earthquake and towards the tsunami. NHK must have sensed this too, because the video clips that had repeatedly been shown – of falling ceiling tiles, and rocking office cabinets, and frightened office workers bracing themselves under desks – gave way to fresh video clips of crashing waves. Over time, more video clips arrived and were broadcast, and the world began to see the horrors from a closer vantage.

It is two days before I am able to draft a letter to my mother, siblings, and children, two days before I can reveal my feelings:

> I watched in shock at the awful images as they came in, at first just shaky cameras and pictures of falling debris, then as the minutes went by, new coverage coming in of the tsunami – those shocking helicopter shots of black churning liquid with what looked like matchbox cars and toy boats and model houses but which were none of these; then the ground shots of upside-down cars and debris along streets that were eerily empty of people; then the great balls of fire of industrial plants and homes and cars being consumed.
>
> That night of watching the events unfold was scary and sad. Scary just because such things are frightening, and not knowing makes it more so. Sad because it was

clear that this was an event of such magnitude that it would surely affect many people whom we know or whom we are indirectly connected to. As the NHK news reporters began filing their live reports, it became more apparent that the earthquake was not the story, and the millions of Tokyo commuters sleeping in gymnasiums and on station floors and in darkened train cars were not the story, but the lost and washed-away people would become the great toll.

Here, in isolation, without a true grasp of the new Japanese vocabulary I am hearing, my awakening sense of the unfolding events is focused on the twin tragedies: earthquake and tsunami.

I would not know the gravity of the third tragedy until much later.

7 章 EVACUATIONS

FRI MAR 11, 9:00 PM. FUTABA, FUKUSHIMA PREF. Within two hours of the tsunami's arrival, the government declares a nuclear emergency, and three hours later at 9 p.m., it issues a general evacuation order for citizens living within three kilometers of Fukushima Daiichi. The Fukushima Daiichi complex has six reactors, each housed in separate containment buildings situated close to each other. The evacuation order includes farmers and rural residents living near the complex, also the citizens of the nearby towns of Futaba and Ōkuma.

Futaba, a coastal town of 7,248 residents, is reeling from near-complete devastation. A municipal official states that 90% of the town's houses have been washed away by the tsunami. At this time it is unknown how many have been killed or swept out to sea. [Later the tally is listed as twenty-five.] The temperature is close to the freezing point, rain is falling, darkness has been upon the scene for three hours, and there is nothing to do but leave as ordered. The unaccounted-for victims will be left uninterred: a death without dignity. There will be no returning.

Ōkuma, a town of 11,159 residents, situated a few kilometers inland from Futaba, has not been damaged by the tsunami. Although portions of Ōkuma are within the three-kilometer radius, other portions of it – including the hospital – are just outside the nuclear evacuation zone and become a temporary refuge for the evacuees.

FRI MAR 11, 3:14 AM HAST. KAHULUI, HAWAII. After traveling 6018 kilometers, the tsunami reaches Kahului on the island of Maui. The tsunami arrives seven hours and forty minutes after the earthquake; it measures two meters in height.

FRI MAR 11, 7:34 AM PST. CRESCENT CITY, CALIF. After traveling 7542 kilometers, the tsunami reaches the northern California coastal community of Crescent City. The tsunami arrives nine hours and forty-eight minutes after the earthquake; it measures two and one-half meters in height.

8 章 MEDITATING

The Japanese are a nation of problem solvers, and their problem-solving talents have been honed over centuries: honed by endurance, by careful study, by skill. I witnessed their flawless skill in the well-built canals and perfectly preserved castle at Matsue: not replicas, but authentic works, good samples of their engineering prowess. I witnessed their enduring capacity in the network of passenger railways used every day: a network that reaches every city in the country. I witnessed their attention to detail in their approach to living in a land so prone to earthquakes, with the national emergency broadcast system kicking in automatically, in real time, announcing the scope and magnitude of the earth's movement. And here, at Iwami Ginzan, a historic site located halfway between Izumo and Yunotsu, are the roots of their consummate skill.

Engineering is the domain of problem solvers, and Japan's engineering genius spans all of its disciplines: electrical engineering, mechanical engineering, chemical engineering, nuclear engineering, and more. But of all the disciplines, it is in civil engineering that the Japanese excel, civil engineering in all its guises: bridges, roads, embankments, levees, dams, floodgates, seawalls, railroads, bullet trains, monorails, subways, tunnels, underground cities and skyscrapers – all designed and built to tolerate the inevitability of earthquakes.

Iwami Ginzan is the site of Japan's most important silver mine. It was first mined in 1526, and grew in importance during the next one hundred years to become, at the time, the source of one-third of the world's silver production. The mine is a maze of vertical shafts and radiating horizontal tunnels excavated to work the seams of embedded silver. The site has been dormant for the past two centuries, frozen in time, since its productivity fell off. Recently though, the site was enrolled into UNESCO's list of World Heritage Sites. These are places that are recognized internationally to be an important part of humanity's common heritage. Globally there are only about nine hundred such sites; in Japan there are fourteen.

As a casual observer, it was difficult for me to appreciate the significance of the site, or to understand why UNESCO bestowed this rare designation. I have been to five other World Heritage Sites in Japan – the floating shrine of Itsukushima; the temples and gardens of Kyoto; the *gasshō-zukuri* villages of Shirakawago; the ancient cedars of Yakushima; the Genbaku Dome of Hiroshima – and found it much easier to identify the special importance of each, for different reasons:

At Itsukushima Shrine, dedicated to the three daughters of *Susanō-no-mikoto*, whose shrine and *torii* are built on piers, seemingly floating on the sea . . . here I felt the holiness of a place kept pure throughout its fourteen centuries of history.

At Kinkakuji, the golden pavilion of Kyoto, reflecting its simplicity and grace in the mirrored waters of Lake Kyoko-chi . . . here I felt a perfection in architecture and a perfection of man's place in nature – a structure and its setting surpassing all else in beauty.

In Shirakawago and the other nearby *gasshō-zukuri* villages, whose houses with steep, grass-thatched roofs have been sheltering their inhabitants from the heavy snows of Gifu since people first arrived . . . here I felt the timeless tradition of a close community sharing the work of the fields and the rhythm of the changing seasons.

At Yakushima, with its two-thousand year-old cedar trees that stand witness to three and one-half centuries of a forestry industry during which laborers toiled to fell younger trees . . . here I felt the wisdom of nature, where the ancient trees stand together with, not apart from, the surrounding forest, symbiotically supporting the flora and fauna of the forest.

At Genbaku Dome, ground zero for the world's first nuclear bomb . . . here I felt the ache of humanity's long suffering over its own immorality and its inability to rise above it.

All of UNESCO's World Heritage Sites are profoundly important in understanding cultural heritage. Iwami Ginzan is the newest addition to Japan's list, having received its designation just four years ago. My own inability to immediately grasp the importance of the site, is perhaps due to the newness of the designation; I expect that over time the caretakers of Iwami Ginzan will develop more interpretive material to aid in the understanding and appreciation of it.

Still, in one segment of the publicly accessible portion, the caretakers have provided a series of interpretive panels describing the mining methods employed centuries ago, including reproductions of drawings made during that era, which help me to understand the story. Several of these drawings show the engineering challenges that those early miners faced, not only excavation and bracing and refining, but also serious problems with water. Mining engineers even today have to deal with the problem of water flooding their mines: water that seeps from older tunnels situated at higher elevations flows down into newer tunnels at deeper elevations, and with no where to go, it fills the very cavities that are being actively worked. The 16th century engineers dealt with this by using human-powered pumps to siphon the water, pumps constructed of bamboo pipes that sucked water upwards and carried it away. The same engineers fashioned bellows and piping to carry oxygen into the work areas, forged tools to excavate, devised lamps to provide light, and erected scaffolds to hold the weight of workers carrying heavy loads of ore. Their ingenuity was inherited by generations of like-minded citizens, and a nation of engineers emerged through four centuries of problem solving.

Although my trip itinerary was all set for the visit to Iwami Ginzan, it was only a last-minute impulse that actually got me here.

Permit me to review my meanderings. That first morning after the Great Tōhoku Earthquake was anything but certain. Although I was 600 kilometers from Tokyo and 900 kilometers from the earthquake's epicenter, I was restless all night over my situation – not from any fear of aftershocks, but rather over the unclear situation with the trains. Japan runs on trains, and trains run on time. Go to any train platform, in any city, of any size, and watch the arrivals and departures: they are always punctual – except when an earthquake occurs. Earthquakes are one of the few things that can disrupt the schedule, because protocol requires all railways in earthquake-affected areas to have tracks, tunnels, bridges and stations inspected for damage before resuming normal operation. Also delays in an affected area often cause delays outside that affected area, simply because railway personnel and equipment and platform schedules are all interconnected and interdependent.

In past visits to Japan I recall watching the evening news after minor earthquakes in one part of the country or another, and hearing reports of the disruption. Those reports were measured not in cost but in time; that is, the number of minutes of delay was the unit used to measure the magnitude of the disruption (whether it was 3-, 5-, 15- or 45-minutes). It was almost as if the well-known Richter scale could be dropped and a new "JR delay scale" could be adopted instead. In the current crisis, with trains in eastern Japan having come to a standstill, and the morning news showing Tokyo commuters waking up after sleeping overnight in darkened rail-cars, my "JR delay scale," by 7 a.m., has reached 960!

So that first morning after the earthquake, when I check out of the Izumo hostel, I feel as if I am leaving my last bit of certainty behind, and embarking into the unknown.

The nearest station was only a few city blocks away, so the short walk was uneventful. The station itself is the terminus for the local Taisha Line, an electric spur route that serves pilgrims to Izumo-taisha. Since it was Saturday I wasn't too surprised by the lack of commuters, and since it was still too early for shops to be open, there were very few other people going anywhere.

The station was old. Very heavy double-doors led in from the street; ancient timbers held the ceiling in place, high above (much too high above); wide planks sheathed the exterior walls; the floor was concrete and just enough off-kilter to make you feel tipsy-turvy; and a faint musky odor emanated from the whole. My footsteps were muffled by the high ceiling and the cracked floor and the cavernous dimensions of the structure.

When I entered, the station was dark – partly because it was still early morning, partly because there were so few windows to let in the natural light. The waiting room comprised the bulk of the station, and in its center a small space heater was lit, providing just enough warmth for two or three people huddling around it, but not enough to affect the room's overall temperature. The ticket counter was closed.

It was hard to size up the situation.

This place epitomized my anxiety. Was it open or not? Would the trains be operating or not? Had the country fallen apart completely or was it just a bit off level?

I found the self-serve ticket-vending machine, figured out the right fare to purchase, glanced over the departure timetable, and waited for the station master to open the platform, which he did soon after. Shortly I was on the train and ready for my day's adventure. But what happened was surreal: while awaiting departure, I was astonished to see the arrival of uniformed high school students.

Now the sight of students riding the trains to and from school is commonplace: it's a standard part of the daily rhythm, and it can be witnessed on any local or regional train throughout the country. Trains become a part of daily life for students at a very young age, and in rural areas I've occasionally seen kindergarteners boarding and riding solo. The older students are typically the quietest and tend to isolate themselves, finding solace in their iPods and headphones or in their Internet smartphones. Junior high-schoolers are of course the rowdiest, using animated voices, with the boys resorting to horseplay. Elementary school students are the ones that always want to engage with foreigners. They find it good sport to say hello and to show off the one word of English they know well. But even this is not easy because the sounds for English letters don't match the sounds for Japanese *kana* so their pronunciation tends to come out wrong and their greeting is invariably "hallo." When there is a group of them and they are in high spirits, they will compete in a chorus of "hallo," "harro," "hello" until I give in and reply *"konnichi-wa"* — which is seldom the response they are trying for.

So a small assembly of students began showing up, both individually and in pairs, walking in from back alleys, short-circuiting the station master who must have known them well, arriving without noticeable hurry. They boarded and took their seats, carefully spacing themselves according to their ritual custom. Now alternate Saturdays are school days, so I noted nothing out of the ordinary about this. Also this was mid-March, the last week of the school year, and these students were probably on their way to final exams, or other year-end activities. They chatted amongst themselves in limited fashion, quiet, respectful, almost somber. I couldn't be sure, but it seemed as if the topic of the earthquake and tsunami were being avoided. The train departed right on time.

This scene, this normalcy, where everyone began the day and performed routines without hesitation, I found surreal. Yet with everything around me happening in such close imitation of a normal day, I could almost believe that everything really was normal. This was to be a dilemma throughout the day. How should I behave? What is the respectful way to acknowledge the gravity of what has happened? Is it more sincere to remain silent,

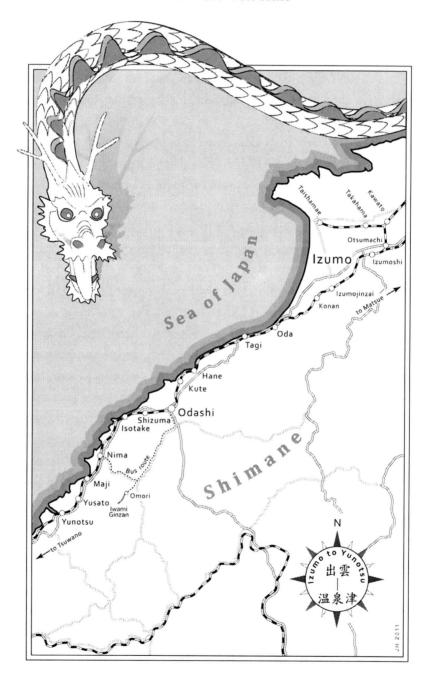

Taishamae
Takahama
Kawato
Otsumachi
Izumo
Izumoshi
Izumojinzai
Konan
to Matsue
Oda
Tagi
Hane
Kute
Odashi
Shizuma
Isotake
Nima
Bus route
Maji
Omori
Yusato
Iwami
Ginzan
Yunotsu
to Tsuwano

Sea of Japan

Shimane

N

Izumo to Yunotsu
出雲
温泉津

JH 2011

58

or to express myself? Do I carry on with my travel as planned, or will that be viewed as being insensitive?

I carefully observed how others were acting, and took my cue from them.

At Kawato, I transferred to the Kita-Matsue Line, taking it to Dentetsu Izumo; a short walk from there to Izumoshi connected me with JR's Sanin Line. On this side of Japan, everything was working like clockwork. At least here, the "JR delay scale" was back to zero; in the space of two hours I had used three trains, and everything appeared to be normal. The sun had taken the chill off the morning air, and activities were picking up.

With this new frame of mind, I began to think that my sense of urgency over reuniting with Hiroko might have been premature, and that abandoning my carefully arranged plans for the day was probably not necessary. By the time I decided to throw away "Plan B" and return to my original itinerary, I had already passed Ōdashi, the transfer point to Iwami Ginzan. Yet, in a moment of spontaneity, I jumped off at Nima, the next station beyond. I didn't have any bus schedules or route maps for Nima, but, as so often happens in this country, there was a bus waiting just outside the train station, and yes, the driver said, the bus goes to Iwami Ginzan. Within a couple of minutes, I was on my way into the heart of the mountains.

Iwami Ginzan is comprised of the silver mine itself, its tunnels and shafts and adits, and the surface land above it, including the nearby town of Omori. All of this falls under UNESCO's designation as a World Heritage Site, and because of this, outside vehicular traffic is prohibited, in order to preserve the integrity of its timeless character. Visitors can opt for a walking tour, which follows the centuries-old trail of the miners, or a cycling tour, which follows the single-track road that occupies the opposite bank of the narrow valley. I opt for the bicycle, pay the nominal rental fee, leave my backpack with the proprietress (who, besides renting bikes, is also the snack-stand cum gift-shop owner), and depart for the mines.

I am delighted to discover the best part of Iwami Ginzan, the part that the guide books have failed to highlight. Better than the ancient shafts of treasure, better than the solitude of a remote place, and better than the forest sunshine, is the freshness that comes from the stream and the trees and the deep soil and the wild grasses, and the holiness that emanates from the very stones of the mountain.

Japan is a land of mountains. But while geologists use tectonic theories to explain the origin of these mountains, the indigenous people developed theories in story form, and these stories engender a belief that certain mountains are the abode of *kami*. A well-known example of this is Mount Fuji. The Japanese believe that the mountain itself is the sacred body of the *kami Konohana-no-sakuya-hime*. This type of *kami* is also believed to reside in certain trees or rocks. I do not know the name of the *kami* that inhabits this place, but I feel its presence.

Up and down the valley, priests and monks and lay people have – for centuries – built temples and shrines to the gods that inhabit this land. Without a map or a guidebook or even a brochure to point these out, I leave to chance the discovery of these ancient places of worship. And over the course of the next few hours, as each shrine is revealed, I allow the spirits of earth and rock and air to awaken my own spirit. As I walk the untrodden paths to forgotten shrines, I walk in the very footsteps of generations past; as I ascend the cut-rock stairs to temples, I ascend to heavenly grace; as I breathe in scented pines and cedars, I breathe in the blessings of the gods.

The grace and blessings of Iwami Ginzan are like a warm greeting from someone in your forgotten past, someone who smiles in a way that lets you know they approve of the changes that have occurred since you last met.

Perhaps this greeting is easy for me to feel because I am now open to receiving it. There are few other visitors today, and those whom I pass are not in large groups. There is one young couple on bikes, one family walking, a pair of older visitors, and a lone traveler lost in meditation.

And there are the omnipresent gods.

9 章 MELTDOWNS

SAT MAR 12, 6:50 AM. FUKUSHIMA DAIICHI. The situation has spun out of control to the point where no water has been circulating over the hot fuel rods of unit number 1 for the past eleven hours.

Although unknown to the nuclear engineers at this time, later analysis determines that the fuel rods of this reactor have slumped to the bottom of the reactor pressure vessel: in layman's terms, there has been a meltdown.

Throughout the crisis the word "meltdown" is carefully avoided by all: by engineers who are careful to hide the unraveling situation with technical jargon; by politicians worrying about panic in Tokyo; and for the most part even by journalists who are eager to use their new-found vocabulary of becquerels and millisieverts. It will be a long time before officials suggest that the worsening situation *could* result in a meltdown.

SAT MAR 12, 3:30 PM. TOMIOKA, FUKUSHIMA PREF. The government issues a general evacuation order for citizens living within three kilometers of Fukushima Daini, the sister complex situated eleven kilometers south of Fukushima Daiichi. The Fukushima Daini complex has four reactors.

This evacuation order includes the citizens of the nearby towns of Tomioka with a population of 15,696, and Naraha with a population of 8,171. Tomioka, situated on the coast, has been heavily damaged by the tsunami. [Later it will be determined that

767 residents have had their homes swept out to sea. The nearby town of Naraha, which has twice the population of Tomioka, but is situated farther inland, suffers equal losses: 770 residents are homeless due to the tsunami.] With this order to evacuate, those who escaped the tsunami's devastation now join their less fortunate neighbors and become refugees themselves.

Simultaneous with this order, the government widens the previous evacuation order for Fukushima Daiichi from three kilometers to ten. The coastal town of Namie, with a population of 21,531 falls within this new radius. It has been heavily damaged by the tsunami, with more than fifty lives lost and more than two thousand of its citizens having their homes swept to sea. With this new order, 90% of the remaining residents are officially rendered homeless too. Only 24 hours have passed since the tsunami struck, and the search for survivors and casualties is incomplete. Just as in Futaba yesterday, the proper removal and cremation of the dead must be foregone, and bodies are left to the indignity of exposure, decay, and irradiation.

All of Ōkuma now falls under the general evacuation order, and the remainder of its citizens, together with the refugees that arrived yesterday from Futaba, depart for makeshift shelters further inland.

Six minutes later, at 3:36 p.m., a massive explosion occurs at Fukushima Daiichi's unit 1. The concrete containment building that surrounds the steel reactor vessel – which is designed to contain leaking radiation during emergencies such as this – is completely destroyed as the roof is blown off and the walls collapse. Officials are quick to calm the public's fears by assuring everyone that this was simply a hydrogen explosion, that the reactor itself did not appear to be damaged by the explosion, and that the release of radiation was minor. Prior to the explosion, engineers had known of the hydrogen buildup, and six and one-half hours earlier had begun the controlled release of radioactive vapor from the containment building.

Later it will be reported by hospital officials that 22 nearby residents have detectable levels of radiation exposure.

SAT MAR 12, 8:18 PM. The evacuation order is extended to all persons living within twenty kilometers of the Daiichi nuclear power plant. The cumulative number of people now under orders to evacuate reaches 139,000.

10 章 COMMUNING

Today is devoted to a quest, along with Hiroko, to learn about *kagura*. Our journey takes us out of Shimane and into adjacent Hiroshima; to a place high in the mountains just over the continental divide. Here there are no villages, just scattered high-altitude farms lying fallow for winter. Most of the country is forested in conifers that encroach upon the road. The midday sun streaks through their foliage in bands, and as we pass from light to dark to light, our windshield is subject to a stroboscopic effect that so easily induces driver's hypnosis, until we emerge from the canopy into bright sunshine and broad valleys, where a late blanket of snow reflects across dormant fields. We are only about fifty kilometers from the coast and have reached an altitude of just 700 meters, but it feels like we are in a different world. The air is freshly scented with pine. It is an enchanted land.

This day, full of cleanliness and purity, is linked in my mind with two stories: one of *kagura*, one of *onsen*. The stories span distance and time; they come together across geography and tradition like this:

High in the mountains of Kita-hiroshima we have arrived at a snowbound retreat. By prearrangement, we have come to compare the local *kagura* troupe's performance with what's been learned from the distant Yunotsu troupe, just left behind. The superficial difference is simple: the local troupe is composed of performers whose members are all women, a unique assembly of seven not found anywhere else. Like most of the one hundred or so groups that perform *kagura* here in the Iwami region, these performers are amateurs. They pursue this art as an avocation, sometimes for decades, while their professional lives encompass all the trades, from fishing and farming to retail and white-collar jobs. Their motivation and loyalty comes from a variety of sources: honor in keeping their cultural heritage alive, pride in their elaborate costumes, devotion in their prayerful dancing, mysticism in the rhythmic chanting and the beat of the drum. *Kagura* has all of this – pageantry, history, story, worship, community – like an ancient opera, played on a small scale, and performed for the gods.

Kagura is a performing art, with players taking on one of two roles: musician or dancer. The traditional instruments used by the musicians – drum, flute and gong – give us a clue as to just how long *kagura* has been performed. All three instruments could be identified anywhere, but they each take on a distinct Japanese character based on their material and construction. The easily recognizable *taiko* are constructed from the hollowed core of a Zelkova tree, an elm-like species with ultra-dense wood that the Japanese call *keyaki*; they are covered on both open ends with tightly-stretched hides. *Taiko* produce low-frequency bass notes that reverberate pleasingly in the surrounding walls, floor and ceiling. The smaller *shimedaiko*, with a much tighter skin, accompanies the big drum and plays variations on the melody. The *kagurabue* (literally, the *kagura* flute) is made of bamboo – wrapped in birch-bark or cherry-bark, then lacquered. It has six finger-holes, and produces a deeper, milder sound than its cousin, the *shinobue*. Finally, the *atarigane* is the hand-held brass gong that is struck with a piece of antler or horn to produce a piercing sound: it sets the tempo for the musicians and dancers.

Japanese music often seems unapproachable to western ears, and leaves first-timers bewildered when they can't find familiar rhythmic patterns. This unfamiliarity arises due to its use of *ma* – the interval between the notes, the silence that is used as negative spacing or for dramatic effect. Instead of rising crescendos, shorter or longer *ma* are employed to effect the artist's intentions; and instead of flourished finales, the music just comes to a stop. I recall my own first experience attending a concert of a famous *koto* player, and leaving in disappointment, thinking that it wasn't oriental in the graceful or ornamental or exotic way I had imagined; it was just oriental in a weird, foreign way. And even though *kagura* doesn't use *koto* or *shamisen* or *biwa* – stringed instruments that play a part in Noh and Kabuki – it does use *ma*. Therefore, the uninitiated needs to find accessibility in the music by listening for the *johakyu*, the three parts to the composition: exposition, development, and resolution; they correspond to the slow beginning, the varied middle, and the very fast conclusion – with the conclusion slowing down just before coming to an abrupt end.

But if the music of *kagura* is hard to appreciate, the dancing is anything but. *Kagura* dancers take center stage when they arrive from behind the curtains. Their fancy wardrobe is what first draws your attention. Made of silk embroidered with gold and silver thread, in appearance it is similar to the finest of *kimono*; in construction though, it has cuts and folds that allow arms and legs their full range of motion. On their feet the dancers wear white, split-toed *tabi* that modestly cover both feet and ankles, and which simultaneously allow them to glide, step-by-step, through their motions without lifting their feet off the stage. In both hands – which are always outstretched – the dancers hold props that help to carry the story. When performing a fighting song they may carry swords, halberds, maces, or bows and arrows. When performing sacred songs they resort to paper folding fans, which they use to graceful effect; or to *gohei*, which are the Shinto wands that have red, green and white zigzag streamers attached; or to *suzu*, which are composed of a dozen or more jingle bells, arranged in vertical columns, in tree-like fashion, around a short handle. When *suzu* are used, they are shaken with small motions as the dancers move through their steps, creating a meditative sound like the rustling of leaves.

The *kanji* characters for *kagura* literally mean "seat of the gods," a nod to the Shinto myth at its roots. The first telling of the story is in the Kojiki ("Records of Ancient Matters") written down in the year 712. As the story is told, the sun goddess *Amaterasu-ōmikami* hid herself in a cave and sealed its entrance shut, plunging the world into darkness. She remained there until one day when the goddess of revelry, *Ame-no-uzume*, performed a dance with such hilarious and promiscuous antics that it put the other gods into a silly state of mind. With this merriment going on outside the cave, *Amaterasu's* curiosity overcame her and she opened the door, thus allowing her divine light to be restored to the world.

Kagura is an invocation to the gods, a call to seat themselves among us. Classical *kagura* has its roots in this tale and is performed with a reverence befitting its sacred origins. But over time – starting in the early seventeenth century – the antics of *Ame-no-uzume* were reenacted by commoners, and the folk tradition of *Iwami-kagura* began, a tradition that reenacts the Shinto myths of the Kojiki. Today, there are 33 of these stories, which are performed by troupes in the Iwami region of Shimane and Hiroshima.

Here in this enchanted snow-land in the mountains, we are blessed to see a private recital – a performance for two – by the Kita-hiroshima players. They have chosen two pieces from their repertoire, one the story of *Ebisu*, the god of fishing, the other the story of *Yamata-no-Orochi*, the great serpent with eight heads and eight tails. The stories are recounted simply, by the musicians, who chant the verses of the myths over and over, while the dancers move around the stage. Their movements follow a prescribed sequence of steps along two axes, the main east-west line and the opposing south-north line; their movements are stiff and their arrangement is formal. The dancers maintain their balance at the waist by sweeping their feet across the floor and by countering their weight with outstretched arms that hold – in these two tales – a fishing pole or a sword.

The Kita-hiroshima players' unique feature, that they are all women, is by design. Although each of the players also belongs to her local hometown troupe – dominated in traditional fashion by its male players – these women have intentionally developed a single-gender troupe, giving themselves the opportunity (in a Shakespearean twist) to play the parts of the male protagonists. Hiroko is eager to see whether or not this gendered trait is expressed artistically in their performances. Are there some special movements or gestures that could be clearly identified as having a uniquely feminine quality?

Today's recital progresses without surprise, but the hoped-for evidence of overt femininity is not discovered. The women's movements are graceful when grace is called for and stiff when stiffness is called for. In fidelity to *kagura*'s heritage, the troupe has not strayed from style or form, and has given us a faithful rendition of the two pieces. Apparently the customs of *kagura* are not to be trifled with, or bent to the will of newcomers: centuries of exactitude allow room for only the smallest of variance.

As we descend from the snow palace in the mountains, we reflect on the similarity between today's private recital and yesterday's public performance. Today we knew what to expect; but yesterday, our first real taste of *kagura* on the stage, was full of the unexpected. Yesterday's performance was done by the villagers of Yunotsu.

If Shimane is *off the beaten track*, Yunotsu is at the very end of Shimane's *unbeaten* track. The village of Yunotsu is tiny, having only two roads: the modern commerce-lined street leading from the train station to the bay, and a single narrow, historic street leading from the mountains to the bay.

Yunotsu is historically linked to Iwami Ginzan, as the port at Yunotsu was a loading point for the silver that was extracted from the mines. The twelve-kilometer trail from the mountain-top mines to the sea, a trail now 485 years old, is still visible and can still be traversed by the intrepid. I enjoyed walking in these very old footsteps along the last kilometer approaching the town. The unmarked historic port, just north of the present town, at Okidomari, still has the smoothly worn lashing-rocks once used to moor ships at port.

At one time, Yunotsu gained some small recognition for its hot springs, and they still bring in the occasional visitor. There were only a handful of tourists at the local *onsen* on the night we were there, and we saw only three of them at the *kagura* performance that night. Still, their presence was the tipping point in the decision of whether or not the *kagura* performance would be canceled that night; thus, we were grateful for their presence.

Hot springs in Japan are connected to the same geological phenomena that trigger its earthquakes, volcanoes and tsunamis. Geologically, Japan sits on a thin mantle: the Earth's crust is cracked where four great tectonic plates collide, creating fissures that criss-cross the country and allow hot steam through the fractured mantle, steam that emerges in thousands of hot spots throughout the country. At each of these hot spots, the Japanese have constructed *onsen* – outdoor hot baths – where local residents and travelers "take the waters." There are so many of them that a special symbol has been added to the country's already rich collection of *kanji* and *kana*: the symbol ♨ is instantly recognizable by everyone as the sign for *onsen*, and the proper *kanji* 温泉 is used only for emphasis.

The water of each hot spot has its own character: some arrives in vaporized form, which is captured and used to heat nearby pools of water; some arrives at the surface in natural pools, which are infused with minerals from the surrounding rocks; some arrives slowly, seeping through the soil, creating mudpots; and some arrives with heavy concentrations of sulfurous gas, which wafts its stench of rotten eggs into the surrounding neighborhood. Health-conscious visitors intentionally seek out these waters, with their therapeutic mineral adulterants, for the detoxifying effects.

In resort towns, the owners of hot springs construct hotels and restaurants and spas around the earth's gift. The owners create a public/private environment in which slippered guests are free to roam the outdoor paths and indoor walkways, wearing only the *onsen*-supplied cotton bathrobes. Guests can be seen thus attired from late afternoon, when the baths open, until the middle of the next morning, when the baths are cleaned and prepared for the next arrivals. Early-to-late evening is the preferred time to use the baths, but many people nowadays try to find times more suitable to relaxation by taking the waters in the afternoon or morning. The baths remain open throughout the night as well, so it is not uncommon for guests to sneak a second or third visit, even after midnight.

There are prescribed protocols to follow during each visit. First, and most important, are the ablutions. The cleansing of the body is fastidiously observed: it is accomplished using body soap and shampoo and rough scrubbing towels until every flake of dead skin is scraped off, every stray hair is found, every bit of oil is bound by soap, and every bubble is rinsed away. Only then, in this condition of extreme cleanliness, is one permitted to enter the baths.

Most *onsen* have several pools of water with a gradient of temperatures – each progressively hotter. Customarily the warm-watered pools are entered first and the hotter pools, for those who can tolerate them, are reserved for later. For *onsen* that have mineral baths, there may be a similar gradient in salt content, opening the skin's pores more and more, thus detoxifying to a greater degree. Most *onsen* also have a cold-water bath, and a quick plunge in one of these causes the heart to race and the muscles to contract, creating an effect equivalent to the palate-cleansing sorbet served by fine chefs, readying your body for a second round of muscle relaxing and skin toning. In between each soaking, guests like to lounge around at the water's edge: some will sit, some will lie down, each person finding a spot on one of the oversized smooth boulders placed expressly for that purpose, or on one of the bamboo or cedar benches placed here and there. Most *onsen* are outdoors, open to the elements (but surrounded by artfully placed trees, rocks and bamboo to ensure a fig's leaf of privacy), and this exposure to the atmosphere's natural state can be especially rejuvenating when warm summer days begin to cool, or when rain falls in splotches on the pathways, or even when snow descends in softness, evaporating just before reaching the warm waters.

I've been told that the heat of an *onsen* is somehow different from the heat of a regular *ofuro* and that it keeps your body warm for a much longer period. I've experienced this myself, yet have no logical explanation for it: it's as if somehow the vitality of the heat, coming up from the earth as a gift, imbues your body with a life force, in a way that water heated by any other means just can't.

Bathing is not a recreation, it is a ritual, and conversation is normally kept to the briefest of exchanges (mostly *oohs* and *aahs* according to the temperature of the pool), even among groups of co-workers or family members who are bathing together, so that each individual enters his own place of relaxation and solitude. The outer cleansing is thus accompanied by an inner purification.

Throughout all of this, of course, you and your fellow bathers are completely naked. This presents a mild dilemma in how to maintain some modesty, which is solved with the permissibility of carrying a very small hand towel into the baths. For men, this means holding the tiny towel directly in front of your private parts while walking around; for women, I'm told, the same operation is employed for the lower half, while the opposite free hand and arm are placed across the breasts to complete this modicum of privacy. Once you've entered the pool, the cotton square is placed on top of your head – for some obscure reason that no one has ever properly explained. Then, when you lounge between soakings, the tiny towel can be reemployed, this time resting in your lap without the aid of your hands. I find all of this to be too much trouble: I already feel self-conscious because I'm the only foreigner in the place, and because I'm sure that everyone is scrutinizing my behavior for breach of protocol, so I find the idea that I could attain any sort of modesty with an eight-inch square towel to be ludicrous.

My first experience with a public *ofuro* was many years ago, when Hiroko – my fiancée at the time – decided that a proper welcome to Japan should include this rite of cleansing and purification. There were anxious moments at the outset, much like entering a mosque or synagogue or temple as a neophyte. Not knowing the proper observances, would I unknowingly commit some sacrilegious act? This anxiety was compounded by the nervousness of being naked in a semi-public place, and more . . . Were the rumors about oriental baths being shared between the sexes really true? I was escorted to the outer door of the anteroom, where the curtains were marked with two *kanji* that I somewhat recognized 男 and 女 (men and women), and I entered the disrobing chamber alone. Then, once the proper washing rites were finished, I entered the inner sanctum of the *ofuro*. That particular *ofuro* was new, the polished marble floors and walls were spotlessly clean, the awaiting pool of water was reflectively still, and no other bathers were present. To my relief, the rumors were not true, the sexes were not integrated; it was just me and the temple of water. I broke the stillness of the water with my toes, my legs, my body – the displaced water overflowing the pool's outer rim – immersed myself fully, and was baptized into a new life.

On that same trip, I had my first experience with a true *onsen* (not just an *ofuro*) after our wedding, when we enjoyed a honeymoon trip to the famous Beppu hot springs in northern Kyushu. The city of Beppu is almost synonymous with hot springs: nearly three thousand natural steam vents send vapor into the air, the city has more than two hundred public *onsen*. The one we visited had seven or eight pools (some tepid, some scalding, some just right) plus a cascading waterfall we could stand under to get pummeled, like a water-torture version of *shiatsu*. And unlike any other *onsen* I've visited since, this one was unisex, which for newlyweds was appropriate, except for the fact that all the other bathers looked like they were sexagenarians, which made my blushing bride feel uncomfortably self-conscious.

On other trips to Japan, we've built entire itineraries around visits to towns that have *onsen*. But this year's trip was not about that kind of purification: this trip was about the gods of Japan and the purification that comes from spiritual pursuits. So, unfortunately we did not have time to join the other handful of tourists while at Yunotsu.

Yunotsu is a fishing town with an all-important bay: it is long and narrow, hemmed by hills that stop only when they reach the water's edge. Its closed end is the port for boats, nets, traps, cables, buoys and all the assorted devices used in the trade; its open end leads directly to the Sea of Japan. This configuration of hills and bay and streets occurs all over Japan. Geography and history have placed a large percentage of the population where lives and livelihoods are dependent on the products of the sea. It is this configuration that has proven to be disastrous presently on the opposite side of Japan.

This night, before the performance, I reflect on the possible fate of Yunotsu. Though narrowly missed, it too could have been in the roll call of disaster; it too could have been completely washed over. I do not know how deeply the citizens here are affected by their narrow miss. Elsewhere the loss of life has yet to be counted, and the scale of the devastation has yet to be revealed. Later, when several of the *onsen* guests at the performance depart early, I wonder what sadness and urgency may have prompted this. Do they have family and friends on the other side of the country who are in need? Our prayers on this night are fervent.

On this, the second night after the great earthquake and tsunami, the players begin their performance with a prayer for the people of the affected areas. There had been some question as to the appropriateness of having the performance with the country in such deep sadness, because one of the pieces would be rowdy and festive. But the troupe director, Taizo Kobayashi, decided that a prefatory dedication would be the right way to open, and that the entire performance could be a communal prayer in support of those affected people.

The makeshift stage, following custom, is in the town's main temple; it is a square post-and-beam wooden structure, elevated the height of a half-flight of stairs, with *tatami* flooring and paper *shōji* doors. We arrive just after darkness has taken hold; paper luminaria line the walkway to the temple and its stairs, and glowing candles within light our way and instill in us a reverent mood. No tickets are required, and no ushers are in attendance. This is, after all, a village of no more than a few thousand souls, and most of those in the audience are probably connected to the players. The beat of the *taiko* has already begun, so we make our way into the temple, remove our shoes, and squeeze between the early jumble who arrived in time to find good seating for themselves. We choose an open spot of *tatami* that is off to one side, directly in front of the musicians.

This is our first real taste of *kagura* on the stage, and it holds two surprises for us. The first is the pageantry. The musician's intro calls onto stage four dancers, dressed in fine floor-length brocade, with sleeves that hang down, *kimono*-style, nearly to their knees, all the costumes gorgeously embroidered with gold. On the musicians' heads are traditional *tate-eboshi*, the tall black headgear worn by Shinto priests, which have no brim but rise, crown-like, straight up to the top seam. The dancers' outstretched arms hold, in one hand *suzu* bells, in the other, *gohei* paper streamers. They move with precision and ritual, invoking the gods to come down and bestow a blessing upon the assembled.

Three full-length pieces follow: they are the night's entertainment. One piece tells the story of brothers and a princess and jealousy; like all the pieces, the story is chanted with a strong Iwami dialect that I can't understand, but that somehow enriches my experience. Another piece features a king, a prince, the god of thunder, and a dispute over the transfer of the kingdom to the goddess of the sun. Both of these pieces are portrayed by masked players, whose facial expressiveness is amazing. How can a performer wearing a heavy wooden mask express astonishment and fear and anger without using his cheeks or eyebrows?

Somehow, with the perfect tilt of his head and the perfect frame of his shoulders, the emotion is portrayed and the story is carried along.

While this pageantry is revealing itself, the townsfolk continue to arrive, further squeezing into the tight audience and arranging themselves with polite gestures so as not to block their neighbor's view. The newcomers delight me: families with school-age children, a mother and young sons, toddlers in pajamas, a group of men in *yukata* who appeared as if they've just emerged, cleansed, from the nearby *onsen* (having sipped a sake somewhere along the way here). The audience has swelled to twice its original size, spilling out beyond the *shōji* to the veranda. And this dynamic flow of ordinary people arriving after dinner, after bath time, after the week's work, is for me the big surprise of the night: a seemingly spontaneous gathering of truly appreciative participants and supporters.

I must admit that by the time the final piece begins, many of us are getting restless from sitting on the floor for so long, and a few have already returned home. So I am amazed to see that some of the youngest in the audience are not squirming, but are paying close attention to the action on the stage. The final piece is the classic *Yamata-no-Orochi*, with the eight-headed, eight-tailed serpent; barrels of sake meant to intoxicate it; eight fair maidens in peril; one valiant god of the summer storm, *Susanō-no-mikoto*; and an epic sword fight. The performer in the serpent's costume has a fierce mask with an elongated nose and oversized fangs that portray his devilish character, and a twenty-foot long tail that he wraps around and around his victims until they are devoured. At one point near the climax, the prop used as a stand-in for the barrel of sake has its contents hurled towards the audience.

Aha! This is the point in the performance that the youngsters have been waiting all night for – their expectation the same as children at a birthday party waiting for the piñata to be burst. Yes, the barrel contains candy and it is sent flying into the audience, setting off a scramble of glee. *Susanō-no-mikoto* prevails and pulls the sword out of the serpent's tail, whereupon it becomes one of the three sacred regalia of Japan: the sword, the jewel, and the mirror – symbols of the empire's three primary virtues: valor, wisdom, and benevolence.

The pageantry and music of *kagura* are thrilling, yet the koinonia is what captivates me – that serendipitous communion between the artists and the audience, each fulfilling a part in the evening's performance, each joining and enjoying the other.

11 章 FLOATING

This is the fourth day and fourth night after the earthquake and tsunami. News coverage has continued without a break on all television channels, spelling out in ever greater detail the magnitude of the destruction and pointing towards the projected scale of the suffering and loss. On this day I float between two worlds, one of dolls and gossip and strawberry *daifuku*, the other of tragic news, great waves, and earnest pleas.

In contrast to the coverage provided by foreign news agencies, the Japanese media refrain from speculative commentary: the number of casualties is reported precisely as counted by government officials, with no one presuming to inflate numbers towards their inevitable magnitude. Injuries are counted using official hospital records, and deaths are counted only when officials have confirmed the death and relatives have been notified. Moreover, the unaccounted for, and those presumed to have been washed out to sea, are tallied separately as "missing" – and this is only partly a euphemism, because some of the unaccounted for may yet be rescued. So the count of the dead, the injured and the missing – as reported by the Japanese media – remains low during these first few days.

Some towns have been so completely devastated that all, or nearly all, government is lost: fire departments, police *kōban* and town halls destroyed; fire fighters, policemen, council members and mayors among the toll. Without a functioning government, and with so much attention going to the survivors, casualty counts will be delayed.

In an impassioned address to the nation, the prime minister, with a voice of *bushidō*, lays out the key facts of what is now a triple tragedy – earthquake, tsunami and nuclear crisis – portraying the calamities as the greatest since 1945, and admonishing people to put aside comfort and entitlement, and to pick up the burdens of privation and hard work. "This is a country that has endured for centuries," he reminds us, and its citizens must prepare for hardship in the coming days, because "This is Japan. We are Japanese. We will endure."

Later, the national government urges its citizens to carry on and not to allow the tragedy to paralyze the nation: everyone must do his part, even if that part means going back to the daily routine.

Now, with these fresh edicts having been proclaimed, the somewhat tenuous normalcy that we've felt the last few days becomes more earnest: life, on this side of the country at least, is forced into its familiar rhythm.

Hiroko and I separate, again by prearrangement: she to return the short distance to Yunotsu for two further days of instruction and practice in *kagura*, and I to continue my exploration of Shimane, by moving southwest into the mountains, to the former castle town of Tsuwano.

Tsuwano, at some point in the past decade, was hyped as the "Little Kyoto" of the San'in, with slick brochures that entice travelers to promenade leisurely along the picturesque main street, Tonomachi, to watch the carp swimming in the streetside waterways, and to make a pilgrimage to the Taikodani-inari temple by ascending through 1000 *torii*.

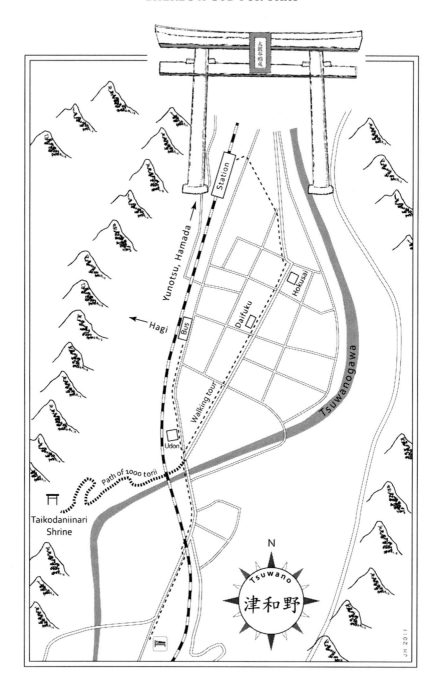

I find the town disappointing. The few tourists that arrive show up by the busload with their flag-toting guide who dutifully points out the carp and the main street, describes the history of the town using anecdotes calculated to bring laughs, pauses just long enough for the obligatory snapshot in front of some historic building, and allows a quick visit to the gift shop before packing everybody back onto the bus, bound for their next destination. Thankfully, I am not part of that experience. It isn't their brief presence that disappoints me, rather it is the lack of authenticity: everything having been too carefully calculated to please the visitor, with very little left for chance discovery.

Still, I have a memorable lunch of *udon* at a small pottery gift shop with two tables and a menu of two choices: thick wheat-flour *udon* noodles served with a warm broth, or thin buckwheat *soba* noodles served with a cold *shoyu* base. Both choices are available either straight or served as a "lunch set" with rice, except that the proprietress doesn't have any rice ready, so she substitutes in my order a thick slice of buttered toast. When the *"udon* set" arrives, the food is tasty, the broth above par, the toast fresh and warm, and the tea satisfying.

In the back of the shop two older men linger over their own late lunch, their conversation muddled by the acoustics of the tall ceiling and concrete floor. I surmise that one of them is either the shopkeeper's husband or one of the ceramic artists (or both), but I don't try too hard to discover what they are talking about — except to note that there is no mention of current events. My mind is on thoughts of the day, and what plan I might follow to make the most of what the town has to offer. While I am thus musing, an interruption comes in the form of two women — one middle-aged, the other a young adult — whose voices are sing-song cheerful in

83

contrast to the men in the back, and who speak to the proprietress using familiar inflections. These seem to be local townsfolk who have dropped in, mostly to get out of the drizzle for a few minutes. I enjoy this eavesdropping, feeling connected in a secondhand way, without being brought into the conversation itself. It allows me to feel less like a foreigner, more like I belong. I always cherish these moments because it's a struggle in this country to be accepted for who you are, without stereotyped images of *foreigner* getting in the way. Tsuwano has had only one foreigner today, and he hasn't looked in the mirror, so it is possible for him to believe that he isn't foreign at all, but that he truly belongs.

While waiting for lunch to be prepared I take two turns through the shop, carefully looking over the wares, which I suppose have been made by local artisans. Many of the pieces are utilitarian – cups, bowls, vases; some are knick-knacks – carp, praying monks, figurines of the local heron dancer; and a few are what I would consider artistic – showing genuine originality in form or glaze. I am delighted to find a matched pair of emperor and empress figurines which have been shaped from the simplest of clay forms and ornamented with two dips in the glaze. I choose them as a treat to myself, and image how they might rule over my menagerie of exotic and mythical forms that I have collected during prior visits to Japan.

Each year on the third day of March, families with young girls celebrate *hinamatsuri* – the doll festival. The emperor and empress are the two main figures in every such doll collection, and they sit on the top shelf of a stair-cased display. The two figurines that I have purchased, although not really dolls, are still representations of the emperor and empress, so I am particularly glad to have found them. The dolls for *hinamatsuri* are formally arranged on red velvet-lined shelves, from top to bottom in unvaried order. Each shelf is typically a meter or more wide, with the whole arrangement of seven shelves ascending from the floor to about shoulder height. Below the imperial couple are three female attendants, who are the royal cup-bearers, preparing a service of sake and rice crackers. The third tier holds the court musicians, playing the same instruments that are played in *kagura* – *taiko*, *fue* and vocalist – with the addition of the *kotsuzume*.

Hinamatsuri displays can become elaborate and expensive and are therefore seldom complete. Each year new dolls and accoutrements are joyfully added to the ever-expanding collection, but while the collection is growing, so too are the girls, and the effort may be abandoned for a time, until they become mothers with their own daughters. So the Minister of the Left and the Minister of the Right may never sit in their rightful places on the fourth tier; and the merry drunk, the argumentative drunk, and the sentimental drunk may never enjoy their brew on the fifth tier; and the sixth and seventh tiers may never hold the royal chests and lacquered boxes and miniature palanquin.

I like *hinamatsuri* because it honors the bond between mother and daughter. In a nation that is so strongly ordered by patrilineal descent, this one day is a welcome break from the norm. Oh, what a pleasure it is to see these arrangements, so proudly displayed!

While in Tsuwano I am privileged to see two of these displays, one at the *ryokan* where I am staying, the other at a sweet-shop on the main drag. The one at the sweet-shop occupies an almost too prominent position in the store, with both indoor seats in such close proximity to the display that a close-up view is almost mandatory. Because collections are rather personal affairs, I feel oddly like a voyeur, not knowing whether or not it is impolite to stare; still, I set aside the feeling and allow myself the pleasure of studying the figures one by one, as if having them pointed out to me by an unabashed niece or her proud mother. Well, the dolls were put on public display intentionally, with guests' viewing pleasure as their implicit goal. So I do enjoy it, simply, with tea and in leisure.

This shop's specialty is strawberry *daifuku*: a whole strawberry surrounded by a thin layer of *anko*, a white sweet-bean paste, wrapped in fine smooth *mochi* rice. By custom, this treat is served with green tea, *ocha*. I have heard of this confection before, but tasting it for the first time confirms for me that its rave reviews are well deserved. So these simple pleasures – *daifuku*, *ocha* and *hinamatsuri* – put me in good cheer to see Tsuwano.

Tsuwano is remarkable in that it has three art museums: one presenting the documentary works of the photographer Shisei Kuwabara, whose black-and-white images capture the pathos of the human condition; another presenting the works of Mitsumasa Anno, the children's illustrator whose watercolor and pen-and-ink technique is used to tell humorous stories; and another presenting the works of Hokusai, the woodblock print-maker world famous for his *ukiyoe* prints.

The Hokusai museum is just minutes from the train station, on the town's main avenue, Tonomachi, in a nondescript building squeezed between snack and souvenir shops. Once inside, and once my eyes have adjusted to the darkened archival galleries, the twenty-first century slips away and Edo-era Japan emerges.

Katsushika Hokusai's artistic career coincided with the pre-emergence of Japan onto the world stage. Japan's closed-door policy to all but a few Dutch and Chinese traders, had, for two and one-half centuries, whetted the Western appetite for all things Japanese. Hokusai himself did not live to see the opening of Japan in 1854 (*that* occurred five years after his death), but his works reached the next generation of artists, influencing the Impressionist movement to experiment with his color palette and intricate designs. *Ukiyoe* was never a style for the educated elite, it was always a style for the common classes, and because the wood blocks used in the prints could faithfully replicate Hokusai's works, their distribution to the masses was assured. Even during his lifetime, the Western quest for all things Japanese had begun, and his prints were sought after by collectors.

The images of *ukiyoe* before Hokusai had, for the most part, been portraits of pleasure and entertainment: courtesans, *geisha*, sumo wrestlers, Kabuki actors, and tales from history. But Hokusai broke from that tradition to portray nature instead. His most successful works at the time were the series of prints entitled *Thirty-six Views of Mount Fuji*. In this series, Hokusai places the recognizable snow-capped cone in the distant background, and the main subject of each work in the foreground: scenes from the daily life of the working class, or images of leisurely viewers contemplating the sacred mountain in repose, or his favorite subjects – boats and the sea.

For Hokusai and all Japanese, Mount Fuji is the closest place to heaven – the place where, according to tradition, the elixir of life was deposited. The immortality that this holy mountain is said to impart was not attained by Hokusai, but the images that he captured have served the same role: today, the *Thirty-six Views of Mount Fuji* are still popular best sellers.

Of all his works, the singular "Great Wave off Kanagawa" is the one most often reproduced. In it the image of Fuji occupies only a tiny portion of the center, while a violent sea threatens

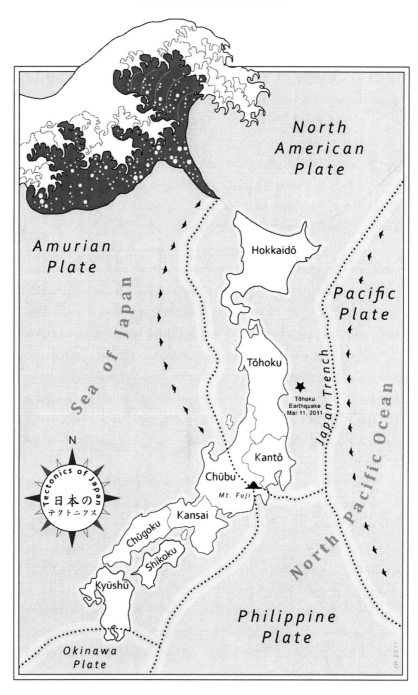

to capsize three longboats whose occupants huddle, cowered, while a great *okinami* looms large, its outer edge of turbulent white spray breaking over its inner edge of blue-on-blue streaked darkness: the terrifying sea a moment before it crashes upon the seafarers.

Seeing this print at the museum, in the shadow of current events, is powerful and thought-provoking. It is still too soon after the earthquake and tsunami for tourist activities to have fully returned to normal, and I – alone in the museum – do not have the benefit of hearing what others think of this print or of Japan's periodic battles with the sea.

I myself don't know how to interpret the famous "Great Wave off Kanagawa." Purists are quick to point out that the *kanji* characters used in the print's title-block spell out *okinami* (sea wave) and not *tsunami* (harbor wave). But, as in all great art, what the artist sought to portray and what the individual viewer sees may be different, and Hokusai would surely forgive me for interpolating the present frightful events with those of the past.

Geologically Japan is split across two tectonic plates: the islands of Kyushu, Shikoku and southwestern Honshu are part of the Amurian Plate; the islands of Hokkaido and northwestern Honshu are part of the odd peninsula-like extension of the North American Plate (which is the same piece of mantle that all of Central America, United States, Canada and eastern Russia ride on). As the two are slowly turning and slipping past each other, East meets West. But these two plates have only supporting roles in the story; the major drama of tsunamis is triggered by the nearby off-shore presence of two other plates: the great Pacific

Plate, which is diving under the North American Plate; and the much smaller Philippine Sea Plate, which is diving under the Amurian Plate. The northern pair of these is what has triggered the recent cataclysmic earthquake and tsunami.

The first record of this phenomenon dates to July 9th of the year 869, along the Tōhoku coast at the village of Tagajō, near Sendai. Archaeological work here has unearthed 8th and 9th century buildings buried beneath the sand and mud. In the *Nihon Sandai Jitsuroku* ("Annals of Japan's Three Emperors") a work completed in the year 901, a story is told: "Some people were trapped under houses and some fell into the open earth and even part of the castle fell down . . . water flowed up the river reaching all the way to the castle . . . the roads and land were submerged, so people could not escape to the mountains, thus 1000 people drowned . . . after that day the farmland disappeared."

Historical documents have recorded large tsunamis every century or two and smaller tsunamis every few decades as the Pacific Plate subducts under the North American Plate. The dates on record are: 869, 1611, 1616, 1640, 1677, 1696, 1703, 1766, 1793, 1843, 1847, 1856, 1896, 1905, 1923, 1933, 1952, 1983 and 1993. Archaeological evidence at many coastal sites corroborates the written records.

To the south, as the Philippine Sea Plate subducts under the Amurian Plate, the record of tsunamis is even longer: 684, 744, 887, 1099, 1361, 1498, 1512, 1596, 1597, 1605, 1662, 1700, 1707, 1771, 1781, 1792, 1854, 1854, 1944 and 1946.

Together these long histories recount what occurred on Japan's Pacific Ocean side. Yet the Sea of Japan side has been in peril too, as the country's two land masses slip past each other.

The North American/Amurian slip fault has triggered tsunamis in 887, 1026, 1341, 1644, 1650, 1741, 1751, 1833 and 1964.

Finally, at the triple juncture of the Amurian/North American/Philippine Sea Plates the record shows tsunamis having been triggered in 1293, 1495, 1498 and 1586. It is here at this triple juncture that the very symbol of Japan rises: the unequaled, eternal, immortal Fuji-san.

Full-time television coverage of the tsunami continues unabated on all channels until finally, on this fourth night, one channel returns to its normal game-show programming. But NHK, the nation's most respected channel, maintains its full-time coverage, and this evening provides an unexpectedly compassionate service: a message board for anyone seeking the whereabouts of relatives or friends and still unable to determine if they are safe or not. I watch and listen to NHK long into the night, deeply touched by the desperate pleas: "Let us know where you are," "Call your sister when you can," "We are all safe. Are you?" The on-screen printed format is simple and straightforward: one line for the name and city of the person posting the message, one line for the name and last known location of the person or family being sought, and one line for the briefest of possible messages. Almost all of the messages are from relatives on the outside, worried to grief, unable to find anyone who knows anything about their loved ones, frantic and frustrated at the chaos and unanswered questions, now more than forty hours after the tsunami hit. A woman's voice, in formal dialect, with careful enunciation, reads the postings one after another: name/city, name/city, message . . . then on to the next one. One full posting each 15 seconds, 250 messages an hour . . . .

NTT, the nation's main wired telephone carrier, has released a news report stating that approximately 1000 exchange offices are inoperable, mostly due to the failure of the electricity grid, although in some cases due to flooding, earthquake damage, or disruption in backbone transmission lines; an estimated 1.5 million phone lines are affected. The alternative carriers, KDDI and Softbank, both report similar disruptions. In addition, five undersea cables that connect Japan to North America and Asia have been damaged.

As a special emergency service, satellite telephones have been set up by NTT in 615 locations to provide free outgoing telephone service from the affected areas.

DoCoMo, the wireless part of the NTT business, has established a "171" voice-message board where callers can post status and emergency contact information; and it has established a counterpart on the Internet: www.web171.jp. When Google People Finder is activated, I dutifully register myself so that anyone looking for me will know that I am safe.

The images of destruction are now yielding to the human story.

12 章 EXPLOSIONS

MON MAR 14, 11:01 AM. FUKUSHIMA DAIICHI. Thirty-nine hours after the first explosion, at unit 1, a second hydrogen explosion occurs, this time destroying the containment building that houses reactor unit 3. The makeshift cooling water system, that has been pumping seawater for the past two days, is suspended. Three nuclear reactors are in peril.

MON MAR 14. TOKYO. Tokyo Electric Power Company, TEPCO, announces that rolling blackouts are planned for Tokyo and eight surrounding prefectures. They report that the unprecedented measure is necessary due to insufficient capacity resulting from the ongoing nuclear power plant shutdowns at Onagawa, Fukushima Daiichi and Fukushima Daini. The outages will last from 3 to 6 hours, and will affect each of five designated zones on a rotating basis.

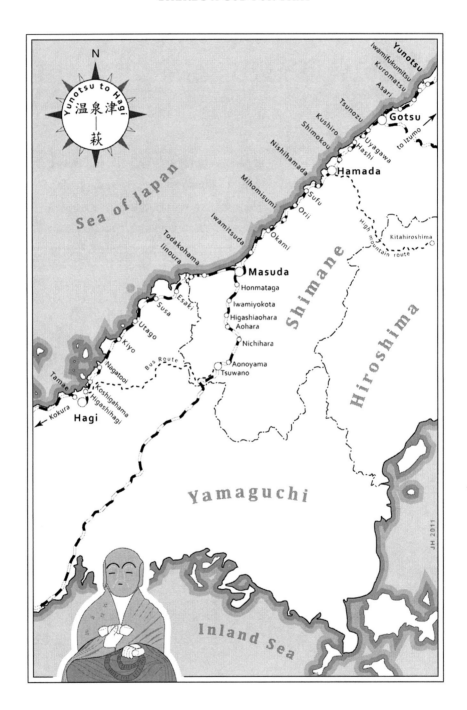

13 章 STUDYING

Though Hiroko and I did not know it at the time, Hagi would become the final stopover of our trip. There we would learn about the nation's rebirth and see the city's famous ceramics, but there the worsening situation on the other side of the country would finally catch up with us.

The city of Hagi is steeped in the history of the Meiji Restoration, and just as Izumo – the mythic place of the gods – is the birthplace of the nation, Hagi – training ground for Meiji-era leaders – is famous for its role in the nation's *rebirth*. Hagi's role in this rebirth came through the efforts of the intellectual Yoshida Shōin, and Shōin's contribution came through his academy for progressive ideas, the *Shokasonjuku*.

The *Shokasonjuku*'s one-story schoolhouse still stands under pine trees as it did during Shōin's tenure, although today's pines are of a new generation. The structure itself, placed just across the river from Hagi's center, is sparsely furnished and humble in size (four rooms totaling just 18½ *tatami* mats), and is constructed with more austerity than usual, even for the ascetic-minded Japanese.

The schoolhouse grounds lie in the gentle foothills of the mountains east of Hagi, away from the city's distractions, a retreat in the woods. Here, in the span of thirty-four months, twenty to thirty students at a time studied and helped to develop Shōin's progressive philosophy; in all, ninety-two men were trained here and later went on to become key figures of the Meiji Restoration in their own right.

Shōin was, first and foremost, a military strategist. His intellectual capabilities were thus employed as a battle waged with words, in which careful engagement and tactics would surely lead to victory. Shōin's zeal began with written defiance of the existing order, but eventually – when paper and ink proved ineffective – led to armed rebellion.

Who is to say where the story of those turbulent years begins? Perhaps the year 1494, a hemisphere away, and the Treaty of Tordesillas, is a suitable starting point. Then and there, the Spanish and Portuguese monarchies, in agreeing to divvy up the New World – splitting in half its undiscovered treasures – would set in motion a missionary fervor that would wrap around the world and meet on the other side of the uncrossed Pacific Ocean. The line of demarcation was drawn, on the unfinished map, along a meridian located 370 leagues west of the Cape Verde islands, the middle of the Atlantic Ocean. Thirty-five years later, after the first circumnavigation of the world, and after arguments over the exact location of the Spice Islands (longitudinal accuracy being murky), the anti-meridian was drawn, and this line, the cosmographers stipulated, placed "Japon" in the Portuguese half of the world.

The Portuguese Jesuits, beginning with Francis Xavier's 1549 mission to Japan, initially had a modest proselytizing success (although the new converts may have partially understood the faith to be a mystical version of Buddhism). Decades later, the Spanish mendicants – Franciscans and Dominicans – challenged the murky line of demarcation and upon papal consent, began their own missionary efforts in Japan.

After a series of troubling conquests on the global stage, the great unifier of Japan, Toyotomi Hideyoshi, astutely determined that the Iberian kingdoms had colonial ambitions against his country, and in 1587 promulgated an order to expel the missionaries. Eventually, in 1614, Tokugawa Hidetada placed a complete ban on Catholicism because, he asserted, the teachings corrupted goodness and misrepresented the native religion of Japan. Finally, in 1635, Tokugawa Iemitsu decided that the only way to protect Japan from conquest was to extend the ban to include not just Catholicism, but all trade and communication with the West. The island nation closed its doors.

Sakoku remained the law of the land for fifteen generations, until 1853 and the arrival of US Commodore Matthew C. Perry's "black ships" at Edo Bay; heavily armed, the warships cowed the Shogunate into opening the country to foreign trade, thus ending their self-imposed isolation. The dominating might of the West – with its powerful industrial complex – humiliated Japan, which had for two and one-half centuries kept to its old feudal ways.

Yoshida Shōin saw that colonization and the loss of the empire were the inevitable conclusion to Perry's actions. Ever a strategist, he joined the debate between "open the country" and "expel the barbarians": Shōin argued *for* loyalty to the emperor while simultaneously supporting the power of the Shogunate; *for* a central government with regional governors instead of autonomous feudal lords; *for* embracing the industrial technology of the foreign powers instead of hiding from it; and *for* beating the enemy at its own game by adopting their military tactics and technological machinery while still retaining his beloved country's cultural identity and heritage.

To achieve this last objective, Shōin took the initiative to prepare a secret letter to Commodore Perry, requesting passage on his ship to see the "five great continents" of the world. Perry denied the request and Shōin was imprisoned for the attempt (the policy of *sakoku* forbade citizens from leaving the country). The technological machinery of the world was to remain out of reach. Undaunted and defiant, Shōin continued to develop his political philosophy while in prison, so that when his sentence was reduced to house arrest, he proceeded to establish the now famous *Shokasonjuku*. Eventually, becoming impatient with the direction that political reform was taking, Shōin abandoned his allegiance to both the emperor and the Shogun, and plotted to assassinate the imperial regent. His plan was foiled and he was arrested for the attempt; this time, however, his sentence was unequivocal. He was defiant in words, even to his death, which made him a martyr to his followers. He was executed at the age of twenty-nine.

Shōin left a strong legacy. In 1863 five members of the local Chōshū clan, disguised as English sailors, smuggled themselves out of Japan and made their way to London to study western politics and engineering. Of the five, Hirobumi Ito was to become Japan's first prime minister, eventually being recalled to that role three more times over a sixteen-year period. Yamao Yozo returned to establish the Imperial College of Engineering, where his advocacy for a strong technical education system led directly to the industrialization of Japan. Inoue Kaoru returned to become the Minister of Finance, reforming the land-tax system and removing the government stipend for former samurai. Endo Kinsuke returned to establish a national currency and to become the head of the National Mint. Masaru Inoue returned to become the first director of railways and is today known as the "father of the Japanese Railways."

The Hagi Museum proudly features the famous Chōshū Five in an excellent film that highlights their contributions to Japan's rebirth. Their intentionality in reinventing themselves and their determination to do this even in the face of opposition, are striking characteristics that have inspired modern generations to emulate them. These characteristics account for how the Japanese have overcome so many difficulties in the past, and are a sanguine predictor for how they will overcome the current calamity.

The Hagi Museum is remarkable: though it is only a municipal museum and is funded, built and operated through the city's coffers, it is world-class in everything it does. The city is rightly proud of its role in the nation's history, and the museum's large-screen theater is put to good use introducing this role to visitors. The museum also has a smaller screening room where three television-sized monitors continuously play black-and-white clips of pre-war and post-war life in the city. Another room houses a series of ancient maps showing the progression of the city's development – from the first siting of the castle, to the growth of the samurai quarters, to the construction of the canals that still survive to this day. In the center of the main exhibit hall is a large bank of pull-out drawers, each drawer holding a unique cache of treasure boxes. These are used by teachers and their pupils in a hands-on approach to learning that emphasizes discovery and exploration. Other halls are devoted exclusively to the scholarly pursuit of Shōin's legacy.

In the natural history section, one exhibit contains a superb entomological collection: drawers and drawers are filled with thousands of beetles, butterflies, moths and more. An adjacent set of drawers contains a cataloged collection of local sea shells: a myriad of the tiniest bivalves, gastropods, chitons and spirulae, each with its own fascinating and colorful form, nearly uniform in appearance when seen at arm's length, but unique (like snow-flakes) when examined closely. All of this is archived and curated with great attention to detail by the professional staff. Yet the secret to the museum's vitality is its *volunteers*: enthusiastic to a fault, these docents know their stuff, each having survived a rigorous course of training that covers the city's natural, cultural, social and political history. As I leave the Hagi Museum, I wish that I understood more of the native language and could sign up to become a docent myself.

Hagi is home to other museums as well: one of these is the Ishii Tea Bowl Museum, where aficionados of *chado*, the "way of tea," visit the museum's collection of rare Hagi-yaki, Kōraimono and Raku-yaki. (Hagi-yaki is the internationally renowned ceramic pottery of Hagi; Kōraimono is of Korean heritage; Raku-yaki are the one-of-a-kind hand-shaped pieces esteemed to be the finest of the craft.)

In form, Hagi-yaki is neither too rough, nor too polished, suggesting a humble folk craft, but its true fame comes from its gorgeous glaze, which exhibits a variety of colors and tones, depending on the composition of the underlying clay. The colors achieved from the feldspar and ash glaze, range from pinkish to rose-hued orange to milk-white. Also, through the application of more or less glaze, the potter is able to achieve a variety of effects:

from a translucent skim-milk sheen, to solid whole-milk cream, to thick cottage-cheese curds.

The arts and crafts of Japan have always held a fascination for me, so it's no surprise that I would fall in love with the bronze-ware of Izumo, or the music and dance of *kagura* or the ceramics of Hagi. And it's no accident that these cultural treasures, and more, are celebrated and alive today; the Japanese have recognized that their cultural heritage can only be preserved for future generations if the present generation keeps it alive. With this intention, they have established the honorary titles of "Preservers of Important Intangible Cultural Properties" – more commonly called "Living National Treasures." These rare individuals (and in some cases collectives and groups) are financially supported by the government with the express intention of keeping alive the artistic heritage that they have mastered. Jusetsu Miwa received this honor in 1983 for his consummate craftsmanship in Hagi-ware. Twenty-three years later, at the age of 96, he was still firing his kiln and producing new works of art. Although I have not met Jusetsu Miwa, I can feel the presence of his artistic lineage throughout the city, through the knowledgeable shopkeepers who exhibit authentic Hagi-ware with pride.

My first romance with Japanese craftsmanship was with the fine lacquerware that is found only in the Orient: utensils, cups, bowls, trays and even furniture, crafted from wood and then painted, layer upon layer, until the finished product shows no sign of the underlying wood or its cracks or imperfections, until the surface is as smooth as . . . well, as smooth as lacquer.

Handmade paper, *washi*, also captured my attention early on: where else but in Japan could the fine craft of papermaking be put to such utility while retaining such beauty? *Washi* has been

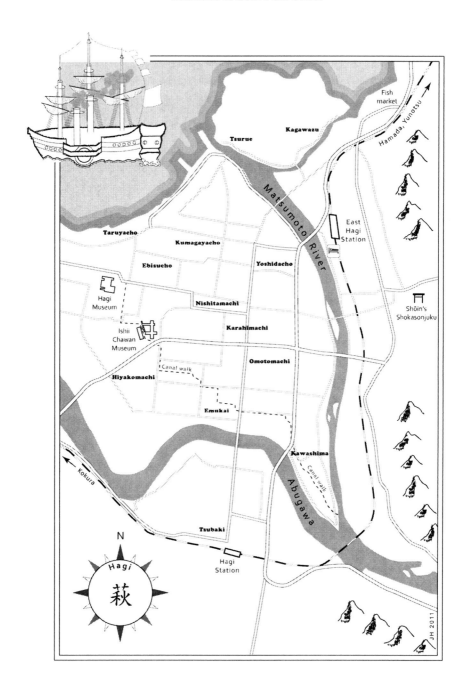

used for *shōji*, umbrellas, fans, lanterns, confection wrappers, *origami*, and so much more . . . including for ordinary writing as well as fine calligraphy.

Over time I have admired the fine craftsmanship of Japanese wood workers, textile artists, metal workers, and doll makers. All of these artisans have mastered the techniques of their craft and embody the traditions of their forebears; they are truly living treasures, with or without the title.

Each time I visit Japan, I look for some memento to carry back, to add to my keepsake gallery. This trip, my "memento quest" was focused on pottery. Tsuwano had many interesting pieces and it served well to whet my appetite, but Hagi is so famous that I simply had to find, while here, a suitable piece to call my own.

Ah, woe! It was a sad day in Sebastopol, my hometown, last year when my favorite coffee cup was dropped. That cup had been in daily use for twenty-seven years, a part of my morning coffee ritual. Its loss was dearly felt. I don't know of anyone else who has remained so faithful to a single cup, but I do know that some *chado* aficionados have passed down tea-ceremony bowls from generation to generation, and that some of these have been in use for centuries. It must be a religious experience to share *matcha* from such a special bowl.

So my memento quest during this trip has focused on finding a suitable replacement for my lost friend, a tall order to be sure. But Hagi proved worthy: while visiting the Shōin site, I stepped into the adjacent *omiyage* shop and found a simple flared cup, handleless, coated with thick whole-milk Hagi glaze, finely crazed, smoothly finished: a joy to hold, and – most important – having a perfect lip for sipping my morning brew.

Hagi is similar in size to Matsue, which makes it large in comparison to most of the west coast villages I've seen so far; still, in comparison to the metropolitan centers of the east coast, Hagi is tiny. The city has two circular bus routes that connect the commercial center, the Shōin site, the castle grounds, museums, and two train stations. As I wait at the first bus stop, a middle-aged woman arrives, glances at the posted schedule for the next arrival, and joins me in my wait. She is smartly attired with dress, shoes, and purse that suggest she is a business woman, perhaps someone with an extra few hours to idly fill before the next train departure. Here, typically, people are reluctant to converse with foreigners because of the lack of a common language, so I take the initiative to break the ice, applying my limited Japanese:

"Is the next bus the red line or the blue line?" I ask.

"Looks like it's the red line. It should be here in five or six minutes," she says. "Are you traveling alone?"

"Today I am. Yesterday I visited Hamada, before that Yunotsu, Izumo, Matsue and Sakaiminato."

Next comes her all too predictable compliment, "Your Japanese is so good." (This is the standard reply to any foreigner who can construct a full sentence of Japanese.)

"No, not really." (This response is never taken at face value, but always assumed to be self-abasement – which only further confirms their pleasure that here is a *gaijin* that they can feel comfortable with.)

"Where are you from?" she asks.

"California, near San Francisco . . . I'm here for just two weeks."

"I'm from Tokyo." Warming up to our commonalities, she apologizes for speaking in Japanese, "I traveled to America once, to visit my son when he was staying in San Diego. I studied English before, and I should have been able to speak English when I was there, but it all came rushing at me at once and I couldn't recall the words when I needed them. I was so frustrated."

I commiserate with her feelings, "It's the same way with me, I can understand what people are saying, but I always have a hard time remembering the right words when I need them."

Now, with only a minute or so left before the scheduled arrival of the bus, we fall into the customary pleasantries about the weather. Throughout the exchange, there is no mention, by either of us, of the drama unfolding in Tokyo and beyond: my language skills are too poor to delve into such a delicate topic, and her assumed inadequacy keeps her on the safe side of the language barrier. My dilemma over the appropriateness of talking about what is happening in the eastern side of the country remains unresolved.

When the bus arrives, I ask the driver for a two-day pass. Unfortunately, I make the mistake of depositing the fee for the pass directly into the fare-box, rather than handing it to the driver. He makes a fuss over this, leaving me wondering what to do, before giving up and exclaiming with that wholly Japanese euphemism, *shoganai*, "Oh well, it can't be helped." My bus-stop companion shrugs her shoulders and gives me a warm smile, as if to reassure me that it's no big deal. Indeed, with the end of the world seemingly at hand, why make a fuss about anything?

Over the course of the afternoon, my Tokyo companion and I hopscotch around, getting on and off at different stops. Late in the day when I see her at the bus stop in front of the Shōin site,

I am the picture of the consummate traveler: in good cheer from my visit to the academy, fortified with local specialties from the fish market, and satisfied with having found a suitable piece of Hagi-ware for myself from the nearby *omiyage* shop.

"I'll be going now," I say with a wave, "Bye-bye."

Tonight, when Hiroko and I are reunited, we discuss the worrisome events unraveling at Fukushima. The carefree course of travel we had been enjoying no longer feels appropriate, and we determine to cut short the remainder of our itinerary. So tomorrow we say goodbye to Hagi.

混

COMPLEXITY

14 章 AWAKING

With the final days of our travel itinerary cut short, we retreat to Hiroko's hometown, Kokura. Here we rejoin the bustling world on the other side of Japan, a modern world of convenience and sophistication, and here I am shaken out of my reverie and nostalgia for a place and a time that belongs to history, and awake to the twenty-first century.

Kokura is one of those cities that few people outside of the country have heard of, but its obscurity belies its importance to the industrial complex of Japan. That importance first came in the form of Yawata Works, a state-sponsored steel mill that from 1901 began supplying the country with raw material for its great civil and commercial enterprises. Yawata Works would later be merged with Fuji Iron and Steel to become Nippon Steel, and the conglomerate today has grown to become the sixth largest steel producer in the world. The city's chemical, electrical and ceramics industries grew at the same time, and the container port at Kokura expanded to accommodate the city's industrial needs; today the port is the 37th largest in the world.

The city is situated near the northernmost part of Kyushu, at the Kanmon Straits. Here the distance between the country's main island of Honshu and the southern island of Kyushu narrows to less than a kilometer. A bridge and three tunnels span the Strait and have become transportation arteries, keeping the lifeblood of trucks and trains flowing between the two islands.

I think of Kokura as the Japanese equivalent of Pittsburgh, a blue-collar city with smokestacks and foundries and ports and railroads.

The leap from Hagi to Kokura starts me thinking about the changes that have occurred in Japan in the last century and a half, and particularly the changes in its religious life.

The Meiji Restoration set Japan on an entirely new course. Everything changed. Political change was part of the equation: the autonomous clan based system of administration and control was replaced by a representative government. National defense was also part of the equation (the country was determined to never again be intimidated by foreign powers): the army was reorganized with the help of the French, while the navy was reorganized with the help of the British. Economic change was dramatic too: with the opening of the ports and the move to a market-based economy, international trade boomed, raw materials came in and finished products went out.

But the leap from Hagi to Kokura was more than an industrial revolution; significant religious changes occurred during this period as well. The Meiji Restoration took power from the shogun and placed it ostensibly under the control of the emperor. But the shift in power was not fully honored, because the emperor's position had, for seven centuries, been relegated to the simple performance of religious rituals. In order to emphasize the emperor's legitimacy to rule politically, the framers of the new constitution emphasized the unbroken line of imperial succession (122 generations of emperors and empresses) and their descent from the goddess *Amaterasu-ōmikami*. Just as importantly, they reorganized the clan-based support for the nation's shrines into a state-based structure. This new administrative structure placed shrine property and their priests under the direct financial patronage of the new central government. Thus, religious affairs and social affairs were fused into one powerful institution under the titular leadership of the Imperial House.

So rapid were the changes that few of the leaders took time to reflect on how to guide the newly reorganized country in harmony with the past. And not all of the changes were good: the shrines would suffer the consequences.

Ambition and pride swelled to produce a militaristic leadership, which subverted the new state-sponsored religion, using it to promote views of ethnocentric supremacy. With this, they waged pre-emptive campaigns in the Sino-Japanese War of 1894-95 and the Russo-Japanese War of 1904-05. A new generation of leaders, in 1931, installed a puppet government in Manchuria. And ethnic zealotry culminated in the Sino-Japanese War of 1937 and the Pacific War (WWII) of 1941-45.

This dark period ended with the Japanese surrendering to the American Forces in 1945. The final capitulation though, was predicated on the emperor's retaining his title. To allow for this, and yet to prevent a recurrence of fanaticism, a new constitution was promulgated, under which the state sponsorship of shrines was dismantled.

Fortunately, this forced separation of religious sponsorship was not as devastating as opponents first thought it might be. Local communities picked up some of the financial burden and worshipers returned to supporting shrine activities on a voluntary basis. Financially, the post-World War II picture began to look much like the pre-Meiji picture.

But other post-war regulations had an eroding effect on the practice and understanding of the indigenous religion. For example, mythology was no longer included in school texts, so people could no longer find moral and inspirational guidance from the myths' sacred meanings; they simply weren't aware of the stories or weren't versed in their interpretations. The received wisdom of the ages became inaccessible.

Just as significantly, the trauma of World War II left the general populous with deeply insecure feelings about their religion. Today, I notice a general reluctance on the part of many Japanese to speak of their indigenous religion, as if the very word Shinto were taboo. I think this is partly due to their own lack of knowledge about Shinto, and partly due to their sense of culpability in having been duped by the false teachings of their leaders. Shinto – and its connection with nature, and its instructive stories – has been hobbled by its recent past. One of the saddest aspects of the modern era is the loss of connection between human beings and nature.

When worshipers go to a shrine they feel a connection to the *kami* because of nature. It is no accident that paths are covered in pea-gravel instead of bricks; fences are constructed of bamboo instead of iron; *torii* are constructed from tree trunks instead of concrete; fountains are rough-cut from whole rock; and buildings are sheathed in unpainted wood. When worshipers walk through a shrine's grove of trees with its filtered light, and hear their footsteps on the path, and feel the natural resonance of rock and wood and water, they are placed in a reverent mood, and good things happen. Sadly, when worshipers return to their daily routine, they become immersed in a modern world of composite materials and synthetic textures. The cement buildings, the fluorescent lights, and the plastic furniture all weary their bodies. And these things break their connection to nature. And their souls shrink in protective gestures. This is a tragedy.

While visiting Matsue last week, I first learned of Lafcadio Hearn, the author who lived in and wrote extensively about Japan from 1890 to 1904. Hearn was not Japanese by birth, but his marriage to Koizumi Setsu opened doors for him, to gather material for his fifteen books. Critics would accuse him of romanticizing Japan by describing a world that no longer existed, but for Westerners hungry for all things Japanese, he provided a wealth of information about history, culture, folklore and religion. Today, he is revered and honored for his legacy of preserved oral history; for some, he is more Japanese than the Japanese themselves.

I am just as guilty as Hearn was, of having an overly romantic view of Japan. I find it all so endearing: the ancient architecture, the fine craftsmanship, the traditional arts, and the polite customs. And on this trip, the instructive stories of the indigenous religion. But the place that first captivated me, thirty years ago, has slipped away. I find myself uninterested in the gadgets and geegaws of the modern nation, and more than ever drawn to a place that exists only in scattered outposts. This slippage, from old to new, is as inevitable now as it was during Hearn's time. The economic forces that have been set in motion cannot be reversed. I fear this irreversible course and where it leads.

So my fervent hope is that the Japanese may be guided by this simple prayer –

As the nation examines itself in the post-tsunami
period, as it grapples with its energy needs and other

112

pressing issues, may it turn to its indigenous religion
for counsel and direction – always respecting the land,
and always honoring the received wisdom of the ages.

15 章 Disappointments

TUE MAR 15. FUKUSHIMA DAIICHI. A fire occurs in unit 4 and damages the building's upper levels where spent-fuel rods are stored. The spent-fuel rods are the waste product from the reactor. They are dangerously radioactive. They have been kept on-site pending the approval of a long-term disposal facility.

Shortly after, a third hydrogen explosion occurs, this time in the containment building for reactor unit 2. Damage to the building's outer skin is not obvious.

A fourth explosion occurs, this time at unit 4, causing additional damage beyond what had occurred earlier due to the fire. Despite the fact that unit 4 was in cold shutdown (for routine maintenance) at the time of the earthquake, the fire and explosion in the storage pool that holds spent-fuel rods highlights the dangerous potential of the plant's storage pools. Without power being restored to the circulating water system, the storage pools are boiling, their water is evaporating, and concerns are raised that the fuel rods could become exposed to the atmosphere. Similar concerns are expressed for the pools at units 5 and 6, also in cold shutdown; however, cooling systems become operational for these two nearby units.

WED MAR 16. FUKUSHIMA DAIICHI. A second fire occurs in unit 4's spent-fuel pool.

THU MAR 17, 10:00 AM. FUKUSHIMA DAIICHI. Military helicopters carrying oversized water-bags, normally used in fighting wildfires, fly over unit 3 in an attempt to drop their payloads into the pool used to store spent-fuel rods. The ongoing radioactive decay of the rods has caused their bathwater to boil and evaporate; without power to circulate cool water through the pools, they are in imminent danger of a meltdown. The containment buildings for units 1, 3, and 4 are twisted wrecks of steel girders and concrete rubble, without roofs, open to the environment. Although the desperate airdrops could conceivably work, the intense radioactive heat forces the helicopter to fly too high overhead, and the water turns to mist as it is dropped; moreover, the gusty offshore sea breeze prevents nearly all of it from successfully reaching its target. The military abandons the effort after just four attempts.

FRI MAR 18, 3:00 AM. FUKUSHIMA DAIICHI. The Tokyo Fire Department is dispatched to the site; they send 139 firemen with thirty-five fire engines. Using special cannon-style water spouts, they spray water over the boiling pools of spent-fuel rods. With a rotating crew working in shifts, they are successful in reducing the temperature readings.

FRI MAR 18, 2:46 PM. It has now been seven days since the earthquake. A minute of silence is observed and the country comes to a halt, in ritual acknowledgment that the souls of the departed have left this world.

SAT MAR 19. FUKUSHIMA DAIICHI. In order to limit their total exposure to radiation, the first set of firefighters is relieved by a second team of 153 additional firefighters from Tokyo and Osaka.

SUN MAR 20. FUKUSHIMA DAIICHI. External power to unit 2 becomes available for the first time. There is a general sense, for the first time in nine days, that the upper hand in the crisis has been gained. Nevertheless, even with electricity available on site from the outside grid, the necessary parts to connect the new power source to the equipment at the plant are not available.

MON MAR 21, 3:55 PM. FUKUSHIMA DAIICHI. The hopeful news of power at the site is a short-lived reprieve. Grey smoke comes out of unit 3, near its spent-fuel pool, for two hours. Shortly after the unexplained smoke from unit 3 dies down, unit 2 spews irradiated vapor. Even more critically, the freshly available power supply is of little use because the cooling pumps for the units that are in hot shutdown mode (units 1, 2, and 3) are all damaged beyond repair.

In the outside world there is a feeling of despair as each frantic attempt to make progress results in new disappointments.

16 章 WORRYING

The deteriorating situation at the Fukushima power plants is worrisome. The 24-hour news coverage, which ended only yesterday, has abruptly resumed – this time focusing not on the earthquake and tsunami, but on the nuclear crisis. Panic in Tokyo is on everyone's mind. It seems that the only respectful thing to do is to hunker down and pray.

In this new posture I feel helpless. I watch the television for hopeful signs, but there are none. The analysis and commentary being broadcast come from industry experts, who attempt to explain the situation in layman's terms, pointing to hastily prepared Styrofoam models of Fukushima's six reactor buildings.

Units 2, 5, and 6 are modeled to show the unbroken façades of their containment buildings, each wrapped with blue-and-white checkered murals that belie the dangers within. Units 1, 3, and 4 are modeled to show the ruptured skin and collapsed girders left by the hydrogen explosions and fires of the past few days. The commentators point to the various critical components at the facility: the torus-shaped water-cooling systems located in each basement; the steel reactor vessels that hold the enriched nuclear fuel; and the pools of spent-fuel rods, oddly suspended in what looks like attic storage. The props remind me of a dollhouse, and the commentators, pointing to the various components – as they dispassionately talk of hypothetical scenarios – look like puppet masters. I am not comforted. My critical faculties are unable to assess the truth of the commentary.

I am not very knowledgeable about nuclear power, and until now I have allowed myself to remain ignorant of the concerns over its use. I have not thought much about nuclear energy policy, and have concerned myself mostly with energy issues as they relate to ecology: damming wild rivers, strip-mining for coal, Arctic drilling, acid-rain deforestation, and climate change. But the crisis of these last few days has catalyzed my thinking and pushed me to study nuclear power. I have much to learn. How is power generated? What are the ecological consequences? And most importantly, what are the ethical considerations?

Finding an answer to the first question is easy. The Fukushima power plant generates electricity using a straightforward, five-step process:

(1) Nuclear fission releases energy in the form of heat when atoms are split apart.

(2) Released heat boils water to make high-pressure steam.

(3) Pressurized steam turns the blades of a turbine.

(4) Rotary motion of the turbine spins the copper coils of a generator.

(5) The generator's spinning coil – located inside the N-S axis of magnets – converts mechanical energy to electrical energy.

The final four steps of this process are common to many types of electricity generation; only the first step, the source of heat, differs. But this is where the trouble lies.

Seeking to understand the basics of nuclear fission, I learn how Uranium's elemental energy becomes heat. And I also learn of the serious environmental and human-health related consequences to boiling water this way.

Uranium is one of the ninety-two stable, naturally occurring elements, of which all matter is composed; it has 92 protons. In the vast majority of cases the nucleus of an atom of Uranium has 146 neutrons, but in some cases (a bit less than 1%), the nucleus has only 143 neutrons; the former is called U-238, the later U-235. The more abundant U-238 has a nucleus which is held together by the *strong force* (a fundamental force of physics), in a very stable configuration. In contrast, U-235 has a nucleus where the strong force is susceptible to being destabilized when it captures a moving neutron. A U-235 nucleus which is destabilized in this way decays into two or more parts – this is *fission* – and the resulting parts contain less total energy than the original U-235 atom. Most of the balance of the energy is kinetic in nature, which in a solid fuel can move only a very short distance before becoming heat. This is the heat that boils the water in the second step of the five-step process.

Obtaining the Uranium needed for this process is environmentally disruptive, and has long-term consequences to human health. The consequences are especially significant in the ongoing management of groundwater and sludge. Traditional open-pit and deep-shaft mining techniques are used to extract pitchblende and uraninite ores, with special precautions needed during the extraction in order to protect miners from radiation sickness. In the mining process, groundwater that percolates into the pits and shafts must be pumped out and isolated from humans and wildlife to prevent contamination.

Another consequence, and a greater concern, is the milling process, which uses sulfuric acid to leach the Uranium into concentrated form. The waste sludge from the milling and leaching (which, by volume, is 99.9% of the original ore) must be deposited someplace where it won't cause harm. But Radon gas, a carcinogen, is a natural decay product of the Radium-226 and Thorium-230 that is exposed in the mining process, and Radon will be continuously emitted from the sludge for millennia.

Yet the consequences of the mining, milling and leaching processes pale in comparison to the consequences of the fission by-products.

"Nuclear waste" is the euphemism most frequently used to describe the radioactive by-products of nuclear power plants. But this is misleading, because it incorrectly implies that the by-products are simply unused parts that can somehow be left alone (albeit for a *very* long time) to decompose naturally. This is analogous to our handling of other waste products: leave it alone and let nature take its course, let the bacteria chomp away at the compost pile and lo, you've magically got soil! This thinking is appropriate to backyard gardens (and *might possibly* be appropriate at dump-sites where we dispose of household, commercial, or industrial chemicals). But the mismatch is that nuclear waste is not a biological or chemical leftover: it is a quantum physics leftover, and it has no rightful place on Earth. Its proper place is in the Sun and the stars – not on the only planet known to support biological processes.

Fission is not a chemical reduction or oxidation process where atoms, which are bound together to form molecules, are split or joined to form new molecules. No, fission is the destruction of the basic building blocks of the universe, which were first formed eons ago in supernovae. Fission does not occur spontaneously on Earth (except in extremely rare cases). When a moving neutron is captured by an atom of U-235, the strong force holding the atom's nucleus together is destabilized and the atom transmutates into two or more pieces. Uranium dioxide pellets that begin as UO_2 end up as "spent nuclear fuel" containing forty-two different elements, from Zinc with an atomic number of 30 through Lutetium with an atomic number of 71. Much of the spent nuclear fuel is transmutated into heavy metals: Zirconium, Molybdenum, Technetium, Ruthenium, Rhodium, Palladium, and Silver. Some is transmutated into solid solutions: Iodine, Xenon, Cesium, Barium, Lanthanum, Cerium, and Neodymium.

Many of the atoms in this spent nuclear fuel don't have the "right" number of neutrons; that is, they are radioactive isotopes. They are in an unstable configuration, waiting for a chance to discharge the extra neutrons in order to reach equilibrium. For any given atom, this chance occurs randomly, but at a predicable rate. Scientists measure the time it takes to reach equilibrium in terms of half-lives. Of particular concern to biological organisms are the readily absorbed isotopes: Iodine-131 with a half-life of eight days; Strontium-90 with a half-life of 29 years; and Cesium-137 with a half-life of 30 years. Exposure to these three are known to cause sickness and death.

As I study the physics of nuclear power plants, I am struck by how many ethical considerations there are. I am exasperated by the proponents of the nuclear industry who talk of "recycling" spent nuclear fuel, as if we could just clean it up and throw it back in the reactor; who talk of the abundance of Uranium on Earth, as if there is an inexhaustible supply just waiting to be scooped up; who dismiss the long-term consequences of nuclear waste, as if it were simply a short-term problem of finding a willing host for disposal; who gloss over the health problems of radioactive isotopes, as if the safe use of *different* isotopes in medical diagnostics, suggest that *these* isotopes are benign; who resort to the argument: "What else can we do?" as if no other form of non-fossil fuel energy could ever amount to much.

And today, as I watch the shaky camera trained on Fukushima Daiichi, hoping against hope that all will turn out well, I am enraged by the proponents who are touting the safety record of the nuclear industry.

Today, of all days! As if!

17 章 GIVING

We cannot begin to comprehend the magnitude of this tragedy, measured in terms of human suffering. The images from afar show cataclysmic destruction of homes and businesses and public structures. But what are the dimensions of the tragedy on a personal scale?

In Kokura, a compassionate scene plays out, one that is to be repeated over the coming days, throughout Japan and throughout the world. Ordinary people, moved by the events, wanting to help, to get involved, to stand together and to support the people of the Tōhoku Coast, do what they can. At Kokura Station, doctors and nurses have formed a line outside the main entrance, soliciting relief donations from the passers-by. The appeal is heartfelt, the response is true, and the strength of the support can be measured not only in donations, but also in the length of the line, as ordinary citizens join the hospital staff: standing in solidarity, lengthening the line of solicitors ever further, simultaneously creating a gauntlet that few could deny, and creating a glorious snapshot of benevolence. At Yasaka-jinja, as at shrines and temples everywhere, donation boxes bear signs with impassioned pleas for relief, while ordinary retail stores everywhere set up hastily prepared cardboard boxes or glass jars with hand-written signs, to collect what they can. At Mihagino's ballpark, drivers drop off sacks of rice, boxes of instant *ramen* noodles, crates of water bottles, blankets and *futon*, large bags of just-bought clothing, and other things that are desperately needed. And pleas for donations reveal the despair of so many who have nothing: toothbrushes, soap, heaters, jackets, boots, underwear, bandages, prescription drugs, writing paper, newspapers, cook-pots, kerosene, chopsticks, batteries . . .

And just as Kokura is mobilized for relief, cities and towns all across Japan are mobilizing, each in its own way, each doing all that it can.

Initially, news from the Tōhoku Coast is unavailable. Now, we have learned that all transportation routes are blocked and all communication links are broken. Bridges are washed out, railways are twisted wrecks of steel, ports are unreachable due to the debris, airport runways are under thick layers of mud, cell-phone towers are out of power, transmission lines are lying on the ground.

For some of the coastal towns, where their isolation is complete, no news of their situation is reaching the outside world, and in-coming news is limited to FM radio broadcasts picked up with battery-powered devices. News media provide an image from Minami-sanriku, where someone encapsulates their plight in three oversized white letters on the Shizugawa High School soccer field: the internationally recognized signal of distress, as seen from a helicopter, SOS.

In nearby Ishinomaki, the city's newspaper, *Hibi Shimbun*, provides vital news to its residents in a low-tech way. Without electricity to power their computers and printing presses, the print room has worked out a system to report the news as "wall-papers," using black felt-tipped markers to write the stories on poster-sized paper, using blue and red ink for critical headlines. [For the next six days the daily circulation will be reduced from

14,000 to 42, with wallpapers posted at emergency shelters and convenience stores in Ishinomaki and nearby towns. By the fifth day, the newspaper will venture from essential facts to an important editorial with this headline: "Let's overcome the hardship with mutual support."]

It is only when outside news agencies are finally able to make it through the areas of disaster, that we begin to see things on a human scale.

In one story of heartbreak and hope, we see the poignancy of families and communities finding strength on their own, in a scene that might be unremarkable but for the details: mothers working shoulder to shoulder, in a school lobby, around a temporary table, turning freshly cooked rice into *onigiri*; fathers stoking the fires of makeshift stoves, using scrap iron pulled from the rubble to fashion fire rings, using wood timbers gathered from the debris of their own homes as fuel. These mothers and fathers are nourishing and nurturing not only their children, and not only their fractured community, but also themselves: they are finding strength and courage in their usefulness. Their needs are dire, and they do ask for help from the outside, but they also need to overcome their own sense of helplessness, and these simple acts of self-sufficiency provide a starting point in their recovery.

In another story of sadness, we see the assembled students of Okawa Elementary School being addressed by their principal. This is graduation week across Japan, but there will be no diplomas handed out to the five survivors of this graduating class, out of respect for the sixteen classmates whose lives were taken by the tsunami. The school itself no longer stands, so the assembly occurs at a nearby school. In the windows, two simple *kanji* characters admonish the visitors: "Please cooperate" and "Let's overcome."

Yet miraculously, in Kamaishi, students of Eastern Kamaishi Junior High School not only escaped the tsunami themselves, but followed their training and drills on tsunami preparedness, and led the students at neighboring Unosumai Elementary School from their third-floor evacuation shelter. The older students marshaled the younger students to a designated evacuation site, and then, as their safety seemed in doubt, on to even higher ground. Both schools were overwhelmed by the tsunami, *yet no one was harmed*. One of their teachers remarked that it was these students who gave *him* hope and the strength to move on in the face of the disaster.

We hear a story of valor and duty that occurred in Okirai. There, firemen working to manually close a seawall gate before the tsunami arrived, were caught by the onrush of water, and were swept out to sea when the massive wave reversed.

Through it all, the government's spokesman, Chief Cabinet Secretary Yukio Edano, has steadfastly delivered the news to the nation. Wearing a pair of standard issue blue coveralls, with upturned collar, his uniform clearly transmits an image of a workman "on the job." He wears it well. As the government's "number-two man," he has appeared again and again on live television, bringing new developments to the press corps and directly to the public. His calm demeanor is the perfect tonic for a frazzled nation. Even while being peppered with questions from a demanding press, he keeps his composure and answers every question directly, never turning from uncomfortable truths, never deferring a response that could be given in the moment, tirelessly working day and night without sleep. He epitomizes the soul of a nation determined to learn, determined to overcome every obstacle, determined to prevail over calamity.

18 章 Assessments

APR 12, 2011. TOKYO. The government raises its assessment of the situation, on the International Nuclear Event scale, to its highest level of 7; this is now classified as a "major accident." In the early days of the crisis, despite international criticism, the Japanese government held to its assessment that the unfolding events warranted a moderate classification as a level 4 event, an "accident with local consequences." Only after seven days of chaos, including four explosions, two fires, intentional releases of irradiated waste into international waters, and unsuccessful attempts to drop water from helicopters did the government raise the assessment to level 5, "accident with wider consequences," on March 18th. Today's assessment, without any new data, is made 31 days after the start of the crisis.

APR 13, 2011. SENDAI. Sendai Airport resumes commercial flights after Self Defense Forces, with assistance from US military forces, have removed tsunami-related debris — mud and water, trees and other vegetation, building material from collapsed buildings, and thousands of automobiles — that had been deposited by the tsunami 32 days ago.

APR 21, 2011. TOKYO. A new law is passed to make it illegal to enter the twenty-kilometer evacuation zone. The villages of Iitate, Katsurao, and parts of Kawamata, outside the twenty-kilometer zone, but within a radiation hotspot, are added to the exclusion zone.

APR 28, 2011. AOMORI. JR Railway East resumes service between Shin-Aomori and Tokyo on its high-speed bullet train after completing the repair of bridges, stations, tunnels, and overhead wires at 1200 places along its 714-kilometer route.

MAY 16, 2011. FUKUSHIMA DAIICHI. Tokyo Electric Power Company, TEPCO, admits that a meltdown occurred in reactor number 1 just sixteen hours after the earthquake. This admission occurs 65 days after the fact.

It will be more weeks before TEPCO admits that partial meltdowns occurred in all three reactors that were in hot shutdown mode at the time of the tsunami, and in all four spent-fuel pools at the site.

SEP 7, 2011. TOKYO. Naoto Kan, who last week stepped down as Prime Minister, reveals what he faced in the days immediately after March 11th. In an interview with the *Asahi Shimbun*, he says, "If the evacuation zone had expanded to 100, 200 or 300 kilometers, it would have included the whole Kanto region.

"That would have forced 30 million people to evacuate, compromising the very existence of the Japanese nation. That's the biggest reason why I changed my views on nuclear power.

"If there are risks of accidents that could make half the land mass of our country uninhabitable, we cannot afford to take such risks, even if we are only going to be playing with those risks once a century."

MAY 28, 2012. TOKYO. Former Prime Minister Naoto Kan appeared before a parliamentary committee that is investigating the government's handling of the Fukushima crisis.

In a statement to the committee, he warned that the politically cozy "nuclear village" has shown no remorse for the accident, and is trying to push Japan toward further reliance on nuclear power.

Kan's stern warning was unequivocal, "Experiencing the accident convinced me that the best way to make nuclear plants safe is not to rely on them, but rather to get rid of them."

19 章 CRYING

Now I come to the part of this narrative that has been troubling me, which I have not wanted to write, and which is painful because it recalls a past injustice. This is an injustice for which no apology has ever been offered. I speak of atomic bombs.

This story has a well-known arc, which my parents' generation lived under, in terrifying proximity; which my generation taught itself to ignore, for all its unthinkable possibilities; which my children's generation inherited, as the promised "peace dividend" of the Cold War's end, but which our leaders squandered. *This story will arc towards some end*, but what that end will be is not yet known. My hope is for the total destruction of our nuclear arsenals and the complete dismantling of our nuclear power plants.

Let me put voice to this hope.

On August 6, 1945 the city of Hiroshima was destroyed by an atomic bomb.

On that Monday morning, 12-year-old Hiroyuki Yasunobu, had just arrived at Kure Elementary School when the white flash, and the mushroom cloud, and the firestorm, and the black rain occurred. Shielded from the blast by the concrete building, Hiroyuki survived the moment of impact. Being several kilometers away from the hypocenter, he was not burned by the blast's thousand-degree temperatures, and he was not crushed by the

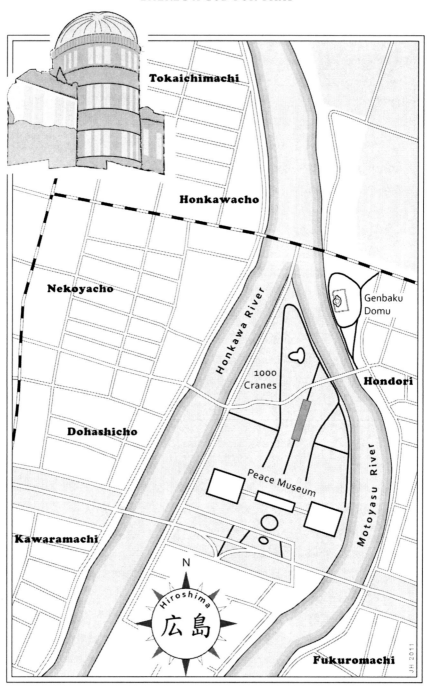

Tokaichimachi

Honkawacho

Nekoyacho

Honkawa River

Genbaku
Domu

1000
Cranes

Hondori

Dohashicho

Peace Museum

Motoyasu River

Kawaramachi

N

Hiroshima
広島

Fukuromachi

JH 2011

132

blast's enormous pressure. But, like everyone else in Hiroshima, he was hit by the supersonic shock-wave that blew across the landscape at 800 miles an hour. It reached him just ten seconds after detonation. Hiroyuki is my father-in-law. Today he is 78 years old.

The great sadness of Hiroyuki's life was growing up lonely, because on August 6th all of his friends and classmates were killed by the bomb. In the days following the detonation, he searched through the grim wreckage of Hiroshima looking for anyone that he knew. He found no one.

In some unfathomable way, he pushed this great sadness down, deep below his consciousness, and he grew, with courage, into a hard worker, creating and running a business for five decades, loving and being loved by his family.

I first visited my father-in-law's hometown in 1982. At that time everything was new, the city was neat and orderly, nothing was jumbled or unplanned, everything was exactly 37 years old: streets, bridges, sidewalks, railways, buildings, marketplaces, all rebuilt from the ground up.

When the city reorganized itself in 1946, the new leaders of the city made an important decision: they would rebuild their destroyed city, but they would set aside one part of it, at its very center, to become the Hiroshima Peace Memorial Park.

Today, at one end of the park, is the symbolic *genbaku domu* – the skeletal remains of a commercial exhibition hall – damaged, but not destroyed, by the bomb. At the other end of the park is the Peace Memorial Museum, which is curated to provide visitors with factual information about the effects of nuclear radiation. Between these two is a wide stretch of open ground, containing various memorials dedicated to the tragedy, and between these memorials the open space is covered over with hard surfaces, nearly all of it devoid of vegetation. Here, on hot August days, the sun strikes the hard surfaces, reflecting so brightly that it hurts your eyes; and the heat of the sun is magnified by the heat rising from the hard surface, making the place feel oppressive; and the open space is so devoid of vegetation that you want to leave. And just when you start to say to yourself, this park is so ugly, how could they create such a terrible place, how could anyone create a memorial that makes you feel so bad, and what am I doing here *I just want to go someplace with trees . . .* then you realize: there was no refuge on that day, there was only heat and thirst and worse, much, much worse.

This is not a place where you go to feel good.

Every one of our world leaders should visit this place.

On August 9, 1945 the city of Nagasaki was destroyed by an atomic bomb.

On that Thursday morning, 13-year-old Tamae Hideshima was at school when she experienced the same sequence of events that occurred three days earlier, in the north: white flash, mushroom cloud, firestorm, supersonic shock-wave, black rain. Tamae is my mother-in-law. Today she is 79 years old.

In a BBC broadcast that day, General Carl A. Spaatz, Commander of the US Strategic Air Forces in the Pacific, said: "The second use of the atomic bomb occurred today at Nagasaki. Crew members report good results."

The decision to use the "new weapon of unusually destructive force" was made by President Truman, who, just four days before that fateful day in Hiroshima, had concluded the Potsdam

Conference, during which he revealed to Churchill and Stalin that such a weapon existed. World War II was coming to an end (the Soviets were on the offensive against Japan) and everyone knew it; the Potsdam Conference was the divvying up of the spoils.

The first use of an atomic bomb was "justified" by Truman, who claimed that his actions saved lives by speeding up the inevitable ending of the war. This specious argument has been repeated so often, by so many people over time, that many still believe the lie. And the lie has grown over time, and history has been recast with this dangerous idea to the extent that now we are told (and too many believe) that our nuclear arsenals are all that save us from a repeat of World War II.

I do not believe this lie.

President Truman never tried to justify what we did to Nagasaki. This is the great moral tragedy, and the great question that no one asks. Why did we bomb Nagasaki? Why was it necessary to demonstrate again, that detonating an atomic bomb would produce "good results"?

Tamae is waiting for an apology.

Indeed, the whole world is waiting for an apology. The radioactive isotopes of Strontium-90 and Cesium-137 released in 1945 are still with us. They have been absorbed by plants, eaten by animals, and entered our food chain. They have inexorably spread to every nation of the world. These carcinogenic by-products are lurking in our very bones, waiting to decay at some random moment. They will continue to inflict their damage on generations and nations (that had no role in the war) for a very long time.

It has now been nine days since the start of this crisis. We are staying with Hiroko's parents, Hiroyuki and Tamae, eating light meals, shopping for groceries, running errands, conducting our lives with the normal flow of daily routine, but with one difference: in the background, the television continues to broadcast non-stop coverage of the tsunami, earthquake, and nuclear disaster.

The constant background presence of this broadcasting weighed heavily upon us during the first few hours, when the initial coverage was of the earthquake itself, and the disruption it caused to the people of Tokyo; and the next couple of days, when the focus shifted to the tsunami, and the devastation of the Tōhoku Coast; and then the shift to Fukushima and nuclear fear. Worldwide, people experienced feelings of shock and sadness and anxiety, and they wanted to watch and learn all that they could, and wanted to help somehow. Here in Japan we wanted to find a pathway that would lead beyond our feelings so that we could move forward with our lives.

I do not know what Hiroyuki and Tamae felt when they saw the images of such total destruction. Did they consciously recall their own first-hand experience from so long ago? Did the images release some unconscious feelings that had remained dormant all this time?

As the news coverage moved beyond the first two tragedies and began to focus almost exclusively on Fukushima, intense feelings arose, feelings that for me were less about sadness and more about anxiety. But while my feelings were born out of uncertainty for the future, Hiroyuki's feelings were born out of certainty of the past. He was *angry*. And even though his anger was expressed in a single word, we knew — as children know when fathers are upset — that he was not to be questioned.

"Enough!" he said, and switched off the television, and we knew that he had had enough of becquerels and millisieverts, and that this was all too much, and how did it all come to this? and didn't we promise all those years ago, "Never again"?

Someone more qualified than I could better explain the historical developments that link the Hiroshima of 1945 to the Fukushima of 2011, but let me at least sketch an outline.

In the years immediately after Hiroshima, the US kept its secret weapon to itself. But the USSR, wary of allowing the United States to wield unbalanced power, developed its own nuclear weapons program, successfully testing its first bomb in 1949. World War II was supplanted by the Cold War.

In 1953, with the blocs lined up along the Eastern European frontier, the NATO allies worried over being on the world's front lines once again. President Eisenhower, in a bid to calm nerves, spoke to the UN General Assembly with a "determination to help solve the fearful atomic dilemma." In his "Atoms for Peace" speech, he proclaimed that "the inventiveness of man shall not be dedicated to his death, but consecrated to his life." (We must always be on guard when generals talk of death and life.)

The *Atoms for Peace* program opened the nuclear treasure chest. The next year, the chairman of the United States Atomic Energy Commission predicted that electricity in the future would be "too cheap to meter." That same year, 1954, the USSR connected the world's first nuclear power plant to the electric grid; three years later the US followed suit. And today we have a go-go-go mentality that allows neon signs to burn all night long, selling corporate slogans to a sleeping world.

Eisenhower's insidious program spawned a global race for "too cheap to meter" electricity, and as of 2011, thirty countries operate 441 nuclear power plants; twelve other countries have power plants under construction or in the planning stage; and a total of 210 new power plants will soon be here.

We now have 57 years of accumulated nuclear waste and nowhere to put it. And this is a truly *fearful atomic dilemma*, because we now know first-hand that we cannot ignore the problem of what to do with this deadly poison. The tragedy of Fukushima is bad enough, considering that three of its reactors suffered core meltdowns, but the truly scary fact is that the spent-fuel pools at four of the six containment buildings have been radiating lethal levels of Cesium in uncontrollable fits and spurts ever since March 11th. The insanity of the situation is that, with nowhere to put the nuclear waste, the waste remains on site. The world is now crucially aware that these on-site storage facilities, always intended to be temporary, are fatally inadequate, that they are makeshift attempts to store double the amount of waste that the design originally called for.

Atoms for Peace failed twice over. First, it didn't calm anyone's nerves: the Cold War continued for another four decades. Second, it promoted nuclear energy without considering the consequences of nuclear waste: six decades later, we still do not know what to do with it. The United States Environmental Protection Agency tells us that this waste will remain radioactive for many thousands of years.

The siren call of *Atoms for Peace*, and "too cheap to meter," has craftily been transformed by the nuclear industry's leaders into the new euphemism of *Clean Energy*, and Dr. Stuart Butler (director of the Heritage Foundation's Center for Policy Innovation) sings its praise with the refrain, "If you used nuclear power for your entire lifetime needs, the resulting waste would only be enough [to] fill a Coke can."

We have been mesmerized by the sirens in our journey from Hiroshima to Fukushima; we have ignored the consequences of our actions; we have lost our post-war resolve of "Never again."

In 2008, I visited Hiroshima a second time. The place was no longer new, but just as before, everything was the same age; after 26 years the town had grown up, and everything was now exactly 63 years old. Only the trees looked different: they had matured into beauty, and they gave the city a grace that was absent on my first visit.

The Hiroshima Peace Memorial Park was now dotted with more monuments, as various groups have sought to memorialize their losses in specific ways. This time, the Children's Peace Monument caught my attention. It memorializes the hope of Sadako Sasaki, whose poignant story has been retold many times. The monument has been the recipient of many, many strings of a thousand *origami* cranes, folded and sent to the site by children from every corner of the world – a symbolic gesture of hope for a world without nuclear bombs.

The Peace Memorial Museum is now curated with a different story. Seemingly the world now knows how horrific atomic blasts and radiation poisoning can be; at any rate, that part of the museum no longer receives as much attention. The museum now focuses on political activism, and with the excellent leadership of the Mayor of Hiroshima, Tadatoshi Akiba, the main exhibition hall of the museum conveys a rallying cry to civic leaders everywhere – to voice their support for a world completely free of nuclear weapons. In fact, the program, Mayors for Peace, has more than five-thousand members throughout the world.

In 2010, Hiroko sponsored a California tour for the group *Taiko Honpo Kaburaya*. The group is from Hiroshima, and most of the group's members are grandchildren of *hibakusha*; that is, their grandparents are atomic-bomb survivors. The group performs *taiko* with an expressive artistry that beautifully shares their message: "Never again."

Students in Hiroshima are taught "peace studies" throughout their high-school years; they learn about the causes and effects of war, and learn how to talk about alternatives to war. They are taught how to be ambassadors for peace. The curriculum is extensive, and the students emerge well-prepared for an indifferent world. Still, one of the group's members, Kasumi Ito, was surprised when she discovered that other students her age, in the towns around Hiroshima, were not taught peace studies. How could that be?

The peace studies curriculum that Hiroshima educators have developed instructs students on a wide range of topics. Using the physical sciences, it teaches students of the consequences of nuclear weapons and the effects of radiation on humans; using the social sciences, it shows students the effects of war on individuals and communities; and using the arts and humanities, it guides students to explore the immoral nature of war and nuclear weapons.

But as Kasumi Ito discovered, having this curriculum is not enough. It needs to reach beyond Hiroshima's borders. In order to accomplish this, the educators have formalized the curriculum into the "Hiroshima-Nagasaki Peace Study Course." So far, this curriculum has been disseminated to 40 universities in Japan and 16 universities overseas.

During Kaburaya's 2010 California tour, there were two especially memorable performances. The first was at the Yountville Veterans Home. This Napa Valley community is the largest veterans' home in America; at this time 1,100 veterans of all ages live here. The performance coincided with the 65th anniversary of V-J Day (August 14th 1945), the end of World War II. Kaburaya's director, Yasuyuki Fujiwara, in his introduction to the veterans, said, "We must never forget the terrible suffering that was endured by the *hibakusha*, but as a society we have moved on. We hope that members of this generation and the next will join us in making sure we never repeat this same mistake."

The performance was well attended by the Yountville veterans, who were enthusiastic in their reception. At one point, in the middle of a rowdy piece, the Hiroshima performers were spontaneously joined by one of the older veterans, who danced and clapped and shouted to the tune, spurred on by his compatriots who clearly shared his joy. Here on this small but important stage, the veterans of war and the ambassadors for peace joined for a heartfelt moment of reconciliation.

On that same tour, Kaburaya performed for my hometown, in the Peace Crane Project's annual Hiroshima–Nagasaki Remembrance Day. Each year members of the community gather to remember those whose lives were taken, as well as to honor the *hibakusha* who live among us. That year an elderly Japanese woman who lives nearby attended the event for the first time. She too was present, in Hiroshima, on that fateful day in 1945. As she watched the performers praying and singing and moving in the ritual motions of *kagura*, she was transported back in time to the sweet days of her childhood, before the bomb. It was a cathartic experience, and was long overdue.

In the program notes from that event, Tomoko Yoritsune wrote, "Of course, many of us did not personally experience the atomic bomb. Yet residents of Hiroshima and Nagasaki live with the legacy of the devastating destruction that the atomic bombs unleashed, and with our ancestors' unfathomable efforts to revive the city, and with the sadness that lingers in the land we stand on. Deep inside, we can feel the memory of that day – in the heat of the mid-summer sun and the cries of cicadas."

That day the members of Kaburaya stepped onto the stage, courageous ambassadors for peace, and opened their performance with a song of courage and hope and vitality.

Their invocation to the gods was a prayer for a nuclear-free world, and their belief that they can make a difference moved the audience to tears. Their voices were clear and strong.

Oh, may there be many more such voices!

禊

PURITY

20 章 Ghosts of Tōhoku

Soon after the cataclysmic events of those days, people began to see *onryo* and *funayūrei* – ghosts not seen for many years.

Now in the days immediately following the great tsunami, many people who had lost their homes were in shock. The things that they had seen in the tsunami's wake were so improbable and unexpected that they often couldn't trust their own eyes, so the sight of a ghost amid all this was no surprise.

The first encounter occurred in Minami-soma, where the *onryo* visited the city mayor. Now the mayor was a sensible man, and he had been visited by many people in the days following the tsunami – not just citizens of his town, but important executives from the power company, and high-level members of the national government – so, upon seeing the apparition, he got straight to the point.

"Who are you and what do you want?" he asked.

"I am Hieko of Futaba, protector of power, source of light, the marvel of Showa and Heisei. I am looking for the good people of my town. Do you know where they are?"

In fact, the mayor did not know where the citizens of Futaba had gone, but he thought that they might have taken shelter away from the coast, so he told her, "Look for them in Ōkuma."

So the next night, Hieko visited Ōkuma. She peered into the darkened windows of one house after another but found no one inside, and this dismayed her: although she could understand why the people of Futaba had abandoned *their* tsunami-stricken town, she couldn't guess why the people of *this* inland town were all missing. At last, at the far end of the town, on a small road that led nowhere, she heard a dog barking. As she approached, she saw a tiny burst of flame from within a house, followed by a steady glow, and then a voice calling out, "Do you have any food? I can pay you."

But, being of another world, Hieko had no food to give. Still, she was glad to have found someone after all, and answered him, "No, I have nothing to give, but I heard your dog and saw your candle in the window, and I wonder how is it that you are here alone?"

"Everyone has been ordered to evacuate. My neighbors left in a hurry, and they didn't notice that I was not on the bus. Maybe they thought I was carried out to sea. I'm crippled and my car doesn't work, so I'm stranded."

"Tell me then, where have all the good people of Futaba and Ōkuma gone?"

"I don't know. When they left they thought they would return right away, so they didn't pack their belongings. Many of them left their pets behind – it was pitiful the first few nights, to hear them howling. But now, it's mostly quiet."

Without finding the answer she sought, Hieko left the decrepit old man, and departed Ōkuma with a promise to send help.

Thereafter, each night, she visited a new town, first Namie along the coast, then Katsurao and Iitate and Kawamata further inland, and finally Tomioka, Naraha and Hirono. Each time she discovered the same thing, that the people of the towns had fled.

She became more and more alarmed. She desperately wanted to find her beloved people, to bring them back, to restore all the comfort and luxuries that they used to enjoy, to make everything right again.

Her nightly visitations carried her farther and farther from the empty towns, and eventually she arrived at inhabited places. At last she began to hear recognizable voices in one village and another, familiar voices of old couples and small families and tiny groups of refugees sheltering with relatives. Whenever she heard these voices, her heart would quicken, and in haste she would appear to her former townsfolk demanding, "Why have you deserted me?"

Each would have a passionate reply.

A mother would say with shrill and firm resolution, "We have no need for you, and we will never return. Stay away from our children!"

A farmer would reply in anger and frustration, "You have destroyed the land that I have tended all my life, the land that my father perfected, the land that his father cleared and drained. You have turned it against me. It is too much to ask me to return!"

But a few of the oldest would be less resolute, and waver with nostalgia, "We want to return to the homes we love, but the government forbids it."

Many days passed like this with Hieko's pleas to her former townsfolk always being rebuffed. Seasons faded one into another and years passed by. Always she received the same response, and the rejections turned her bitter.

At this same time, apparitions of another sort were occurring. People all along the Tōhoku coast to the north began to tell of nightly encounters with a particular *funayūrei*.

Now this *funayūrei* was similar in appearance to the *onryo* of the south. Both were dressed in full-length white *kimono*, draped in folds from their shoulders, and loose about the waist. Both allowed their long, black hair to fall unrestrained and unkempt. And both had that unmistakable peculiarity that identified them as visitors from *anoyo*, the other side – they never touched the ground, their feet and legs could not be seen, the lower half of the body dissolved into the air, transparently losing its form.

But despite the similarities in appearance, this ghost of the north came from a different place and came for a different purpose. The other ghost – the ghost of the south – came from purgatory, a place of wandering anxiety, where troubled souls seek resolution and redemption. This ghost – the ghost of the north – came from the deep waters of the sea, where souls are bathed in eternal blessings of honor and remembrance.

Now on the night after the tsunami, this *funayūrei* visited Koki Kato, the mayor of Ōtsuchi. The mayor was an energetic man, well organized, and capable in his leadership. The fact that the mayor was dead, did not deter the ghost. His death had occurred like this: immediately after the earth stopped shaking, Kato called an emergency meeting at the city's municipal building, establishing a command post, while engineers surveyed the building for structural damage. When he saw the approaching tsunami, he directed his staff to hurry from the second floor to the roof, but his actions were not in time to save his own life. He was washed out to sea.

Knowing of this, the *funayūrei* approached the mayor to ask for his help with the effort that she was about to embark upon, and said, "Kato-san, will you help me in my quest?"

He asked, "Who are you, and what do you want?"

"I am Fumie of Nihon Kaiko, messenger of the sea, and patron of all who have drowned. I have come to guide the souls of this place to the great sea palace east of Jodogahama."

Because the mayor's life was defined by service to others, he thought it would be an honor to have his first act in the new world be a helpful gesture, so he asked, "What do you need, and how can I help?"

She answered, "I must gather all the souls that were swept to sea and invite them to take their rightful place in the sea palace."

Now Kato's sense of duty was strong and he wanted to help, but he had to state the obvious, "How can I help when I am dead?"

"Oh," she replied, "you will find a way, you always do."

So he agreed, despite his own feelings on the matter. Before he departed to begin this work, Fumie left him with these special instructions: "When you find the lost souls you must invite them to the sea palace at Jodogahama, where they will be the first to see *Amaterasu-ōmikami* awake each morning, and the first to feel her warm radiance. But you must have their consent – if they want to return to their homeland to be closer to their relatives, you must obey their wishes. And remember, we have only seven days until *shonanoka*."

The task that Kato had been given was great because there were many thousands of souls to find. So the mayor, ever efficient, began by searching for former members of the government who also had died in the tsunami. He was able to locate hundreds: council members, city engineers, clerks, fire fighters, policemen, teachers, and hospital workers. They came from every town along the coast, each with a unique story, yet all of them united by the common circumstance of their deaths. He assembled all these souls on the second night and prepared his most important speech ever.

He spoke solemnly to the assembly: "Fumie of Nihon Kaiko, messenger of the sea, and patron of all who have drowned, has asked for our help. I repeat her request: Find the lost souls of our towns, and help them to reach their final resting place. When you find them, you must invite them to retire to the sea palace in the east, but if they decline and wish to return to their homeland, you must help them return."

All in the assembly felt duty-bound to carry out this last and most important official duty, but they wondered about themselves. One of them ventured to ask, "And what about us, are we also to choose our final resting place?"

Kato assured them that they too would be granted the choice of a final resting place.

So the appointed servants arose, and for the next five days and five nights they could be seen by the living: hundreds of ghostly forms fulfilling their duty. And over land and sea, fiery *hitodama* were seen here and there, as each soul departed its earthly body, each having made the final choice. And along the coast, thousands of bodies washed ashore, returned by the sea, in fulfillment of Fumie's orders that any who wished to return to land must be granted that final wish.

On the seventh day, *shonanoka* rites were observed.

Kato and the appointed servants had fulfilled their duty. Kato returned to Fumie and said, "We have done all that you have asked. We have contacted the restless souls and offered our guidance. They are now in their final resting places."

She thanked him for his diligence, "You have worked under extreme conditions with no thought for yourself. The survivors have been wailing and crying for seven days and seven nights. But now they can grieve properly, knowing that their loved ones' journey to *anoyo* is complete.

"And as for you Kato-san, what is your final wish?" she asked.

"I belong with my family and my community. I wish to be returned to land."

The next day, Kato's body washed ashore, having been carried by the current some distance down the coast. His body was carefully washed and wrapped in white linen, all of the proper rites were performed, and cremation was carried out according to custom.

Fumie returned to the great sea palace at Jodogahama, and the apparitions along the coast ceased.

But in the south, the homeless refugees of Fukushima continued to be visited by Hieko. Night after night she pleaded with the former townsfolk to return, promising them a new future, a future that would be even safer than before.

But they could not be persuaded. Pointing to Futaba's once proud slogan, "Nuclear Power Is the Energy of a Bright Tomorrow," they shook their heads. How could they ever believe that again?

So Hieko became a bitter, mad woman. She retreated to the glowing core of the exclusion zone, where she huddled over her still radiant treasure, which had become a liquid pool of silver-white Cesium. There she remained for untold years, suspended in despair, unable to find a single living soul to keep her company.

Meanwhile all along the coast to the north, people began rebuilding their lives and their towns. Five times they planted the fields and five times they harvested the rice. The rhythm of life had begun to return, and there was a general call by the people to celebrate their efforts.

Now in the seventh month of the year, from the 13th to the 15th day of the month, the traditional festival of *obon* is held throughout the land. These are the nights when the dead rise and mingle with the living. *Obon* is the festival to welcome the returning souls and to honor their memory.

So in the seventh month of the fifth year, the residents of Matsushima hosted a splendid outdoor *bon odori*, a full day and night of the grandest celebration. *Amaterasu-ōmikami* shone that day with a radiance seldom seen; she sent warm rays of glory upon the early arrivals, which placed everyone in a festive mood. The summer fields of rice had ripened to a golden hue, scenting the air with a toasty, nutty aroma of grass and tea. Above, dragonflies hovered in lazy circles seeking a landing spot, while below, in the harvested fields, crickets scoured the ground for fallen kernels, and if you listened carefully you could hear them, creaking like old floorboards.

The dragonflies and crickets played back-beat while the cicadas carried the tune: first the double basses and cellos, then the violas, and finally the violins, a cicada concerto on the swelling summer air, a sound that on any other day would have been as annoying as kazoos, but on this particular day was a sweet harbinger of the musicians to come. Only the crows complained (but no one listened to them anyway), and the buzz and hum of the fields could be felt throughout the city, quickening its tempo.

Merchants set up stalls all along the perimeter of the bay-side park, each square stall just large enough for a cook, each skirted with patriotic red-and-white striped banners and edged with *noren* that spelled out the items for sale. The stalls were bunched together, carnival fashion, in a long line that curved around the bay – hundreds, maybe more, seemingly going on forever. The buzz and hum of the fields gave way to the sounds and smells of the food stalls –

> Deep fryers
> were crackling with seafood –
> *ikayaki, takoyaki,*
> *ayu, oden.*

> Portable grills
> were sizzling with meats –
> *yakiniku, yakitori*
> *karaage.*

> Hotplates were
> hissing with roots and shoots –
> *jyagabata, okonomiyaki,*
> *atsuage.*

> Vendors sold
> old-time festival sweets –
> *kaki-kōri, imagawayaki,*
> *dango.*

And soon the hawkers began to ply the growing crowd, with shouts of "Welcome, welcome, wel...come!"

By mid-afternoon the townspeople filled the promenade and choice spots in the park. Many people arrived together, young families with children and extended families with grandparents, but before long they split into groups segregated by age and gender – except the smallest of children who stayed with their mothers. The preschoolers ran in circles chasing and being chased, sensing the festive mood in the air, testing the limits of their boundaries and fresh freedom. Young boys sneaked away to the water's edge to play with fireworks, unaware that their watchful parents were monitoring their safety. Adolescent girls, in groups of three and four, cruised the food stalls, seeking out remembered favorites; tasting, sharing, comparing, before settling on this sweet or that; and all the while showing off their bright summer *yukata*, and their new-found maturity. Fathers found old chums and drank *sake*, even while retaining their role as patriarchs, dispatching one family member and another to get this or that. And seniors – in joy at the full spectacle – watched how each generation followed, one after the other, in progressive order, as it should be.

Everything was in place for a great celebration, and the townsfolk felt in their hearts that the hard work of rebuilding their town had been worthwhile. When their thoughts turned back to the day of the tsunami, they reflected upon their losses, and ached to share this glorious rebirth with their missing loved ones. And their hopes became dreams, and their dreams began to take form, and their longing was heard on the other side, in *anoyo*, by the souls of their loved ones.

At the appointed evening hour, the deep sound of the temple's *bonsho* could be heard coming from the cedars. The bell was struck 108 times, slowly, with enough time between each note to pray – the resonance not imposing but inviting, awakening all sentient beings, and calling for their release from suffering.

On that day, in the seventh month of the fifth year, the bell resounded farther than ever before, carried by the hopes and dreams and longings of the assembled. And it was heard throughout the land: it reached the resting places of the departed, not only the souls of that fateful day five years earlier, but the souls of their ancestors, and the souls of the long-forgotten as well. And all these souls awakened and heeded the call.

Finally, *Amaterasu* parted from Matsushima, to rest. Her departure was painted, for the longest time, with pink and cream pastels; until gradually her glory began to fade, deepening into the steel and charcoal of night. The mood of the crowd changed, the excitement of the afternoon's activities slowed to a more measured pace, children found their way back to their parents, and parents prepared their families for the events to come.

Now on that night, *Tsukuyomi-no-mikoto* was nearing his fullness, and he arrived for the celebration shortly after his sister *Amaterasu* had departed. *Tsukuyomi's* nature was much softer than his sister's, which was a relief for the townsfolk (for *Amaterasu's* heat and glare had worn out its welcome). *Tsukuyomi's* reflective nature enhanced the reflective mood that was descending upon the assembled community.

All 108 notes of the *bonsho* had been issued, and a calm resonated throughout the gathered throng. Each family, reunited, reposed in loose attire, quietly recalled memories of other *obon*, and waited for this night's *odori* to begin.

It began like this: from the cedars of Zuiganji, a procession
of musicians emerged, and they walked, in stately form, past
moss-covered rocks, through the temple's great outer gate, and on
toward the designated place, on the shore of Matsushima Bay, to
the awaiting crowd. At the lead, a single *fue* played a shrill song
of plaintive longing, and it pierced the darkness with its cry of
sadness. Next, an *okedaiko*, with tightly stretched drum-heads,
beat out the marching rhythm, moving the procession forward
with its measured notes. The procession moved past the street
vendors and past the waiting crowd and on toward the awaiting
yagura, where lanterns were hung, lighting the night, creating a
space of expectation, a place where the possibilities of magic and
fantasy would occur. And as the musicians and singers reached
the stage, the townsfolk took their cue, and formed a large circle,
with the players at its center.

Now the *fue* stopped and the *taiko* caught the tempo. As the
tune changed from sorrow to resolve, the gathering took their
first steps of the night. The dancers moved counterclockwise in
unison, ever so slowly . . .

That first dance, *obon-no-uta*, was followed by others with
similar rhythms, and the hands of the dancers made gestures of
capture and release. More dances followed – with the musicians
gradually beating bolder and louder and faster, and the singers
conveying ever more joy in their songs.

The dances were led by the guardians of tradition, whose
responsibility it was to remember from year to year the movements of each dance. They performed their role with grace and
beauty. Their bodies swayed like flowers in a light breeze, and the
floral patterns of their colorful *yukata* reinforced the impression

that this was indeed a garden of beauty: human form in inspired imitation of nature.

Mothers were especially careful to instill in their young daughters the ritual of dance. Thus, the adolescent girls who had brought such charm to the afternoon, brought hope and beauty to the evening as well. And the guardians of tradition, who not only knew the steps and movements of each dance, but also embodied the fullness of each gesture, brought to life the sanctity of the night.

As the night reached its balance, men who knew the steps were no longer content to watch from the side, and even young boys, whose inhibitions had kept them away, heeded the beckoning call.

So it happened that amid this joy, the ghosts of Tōhoku – awakened by the *bonsho's* tolling, and arriving on the wings of *hotaru* – alighted upon the festival grounds.

Spirits from near and afar arrived, thousands upon thousands heeding the call. Transmogrified to earthly form, they joined the dance. The circles grew as the living and the dead, now intermingling, swayed in unified motions.

Everyone who died on that tragic day arrived, from every coastal city of Miyagi and Iwate and Fukushima and beyond.

Among them were the sixteen graduates of Okawa Elementary School, proudly holding their posthumous diplomas, together with siblings and friends from the lower grades: 74 spirits in all. They wore brightly colored *yukata*, and when the Home Run Ondo was performed, they ran the bases, racing past parents and teachers, with playful glee.

All the spirits of the firemen from that day were there: 27 professionals accompanied by 249 volunteers.

The former mayor of Ōtsuchi, Koki Kato, was there, leading the contingent of government workers in the *Heisei Ondo*.

And so great was the invocation, that it spanned distance and time: the call was heeded by spirits from the far side of Japan, and from times that had long ago faded. Even spirits long since transformed into household ancestors and Buddhas heeded the call.

The magic of those hours conjured Shōin and the Chōshū Five who arrived from Hagi in formal samurai attire. And former generations of *kagura* dancers made their appearance with their embroidered costumes and expressive wooden masks. Even the Minister of the Left and the Minister of the Right found their way, and shared a toast of *sake* – poured by the imperial cup bearers – with the merry drunk, the argumentative drunk, and the sentimental drunk of *hinamatsuri* fame. The magic reached across time to the miners of Iwami Ginzan who delighted in joining in everyone's all-time favorite, *tanko-bushi*.

Even Hokusai was there, sitting to one side of the action, sketching with fine strokes, capturing the scene in all its detail: the *yagura* at the center, the glow of the festival lanterns, the circles of dancing forms, and the reflective waters of the bay.

Long into the night they danced, the living and the dead, sharing magical moments of reunion and remembrance . . . moments that brought promise and hope for the future . . . moments that carried resolve and purpose in life . . . moments that checked anxieties and brought inner calm.

When the music of the final dance began, the tempo slowed, the living took on a solemnity befitting the final hour, and the dead graciously announced their imminent departure. *Obon-no-uta* was performed in bittersweet reverence.

The living, now recharged with hope in the future, were ready to bid farewell to the spirits, and were ready to live their lives with new resolve.

Finally, at the hour of departure, when the dancing had stopped, the ghosts of Tōhoku shed their earthly forms. Paper lanterns had been prepared, in accordance with the *tōrō nagashi* custom, for their conveyance to *takama-no-hara*, the dwelling place of the gods.

Families with children led the way, marching with lanterns to the shores of Matsushima Bay. Others followed, each carrying a precious spirit-filled vessel, in solemn procession. There, at the water's edge, in the lee of Fukuura Island, at the temple of Godaido, the lanterns were set adrift, each cradling a cherished soul to be released upon its journey. And the lanterns thus afloat – thousands upon thousands – cast a warm glow over the sea.

Kami

Amaterasu-ōmikami is the goddess of the sun, and ancestral deity of the imperial family. She is the most important *kami* in the Shinto pantheon. She is the sister of *Tsukuyomi* and *Susanō*.

Ame-no-uzume is the goddess of sensuality and revelry. Because of her role in enticing the sun goddess to reveal herself, she is also considered the goddess of dawn.

Benzaiten is the water goddess and patroness of learning, art, music, poetry, rhetoric, eloquence, and all "things that flow." She is originally a Buddhist goddess, but she has been adopted into the Shinto pantheon under the name *Itsukushima-hime*.

Ebisu is the god of good fortune, and is the patron of fishermen and workmen. He is known as the laughing god.

Konohana-no-sakuya-hime is the goddess of Mount Fuji, which is the spiritual symbol of the nation. Her name is an allusion to the ephemeral beauty of the cherry blossom.

Ōkuninushi-no-mikoto was the original ruler of Earth, but when *Ninigi* was sent to replace him, *Ōkuninushi* was made ruler of the unseen world. He is the patron of good fortune and good marital relationships.

Susanō-no-mikoto is the Ferocious Virulent Male God, patron of the summer storm. He is the brother of *Tsukuyomi* and *Amaterasu*.

Tsukuyomi-no-mikoto is the god of the moon. He is the brother of *Amaterasu* and *Susanō*.

Glossary

Some of the Japanese words in this book may be familiar to you; for example, words like *kimono* and *origami* enjoy widespread usage. But many of the Japanese words are unfamiliar to English speakers, and their translation – when not provided adequately within the text – is provided here.

In the Japanese language, nouns do not have singular and plural forms, thus it is a mistake to add an /s/ at the end of a word like *kami*. Plurality is inferred by context.

anko [an·ko] A sweet red paste made from the beans of the *azuki* bush (*Vigna angularis*).

anoyo [a·no·yo] The afterlife. *Konoyo* and *anoyo* are the spiritual dimensions for this life and the afterlife, derived from the common adverbs *kono* and *ano*, literally, "here" and "there".

arame [a·ra·me] A dark-brown, semi-sweet kelp, used as a garnish.

arigato [a·ri·ga·to] Thank you.

atarigane [a·ta·ri·ga·ne] A hand-held brass gong.

atsuage [a·tsu·a·ge] Fried tofu.

ayu [a·yu] Sweet smelts.

biwa [bi·wa] A short-necked fretted lute, often used to accompany storytelling.

bon odori [bo·n·o·do·ri] A contracted form of the words *obon odori*.

bonsho [bon·sho] An enormous cast bronze bell struck sideways with a heavy wooden ramrod.

bushidō [bu·shi·do·o] The traditional Japanese moral code of frugality, self-sacrifice, loyalty, obedience, duty and honor.

butsudan [bu·tsu·dan] A small household shrine that holds religious icons and statues.

chado [cha·do] Japanese tea ceremony.

daifuku [da·i·fu·ku] A confection made of fresh pounded rice filled with *anko*; they are more commonplace and less expensive than *wagashi*.

daikon [da·i·kon] A long, fat, white radish.

dango [dan·go] Rice flour dumplings with soy sauce.

fue [fu·e] The generic name for a bamboo flute; *shinobue* and *kagurabue* are two examples.

fukinotō [fu·ki·no·to·o] Fresh butter-bur buds, a bog rhubarb.

funayūrei [fu·na·yu·u·re·i] Spirits of the sea that lure victims to death by drowning.

futon [fu·ton] A mattress of cotton batting.

gaijin [ga·i·jin] A foreigner.

gasshō-zukuri [ga·sho·o·zu·ku·ri] An architectural style where the steep roofs have an appearance of two hands joined in prayer.

geisha [ge·i·sha] A female entertainer trained in classical music and dance.

genbaku domu [gen·ba·ku·do·mu] The building whose skeletal remains mark Hiroshima's ground zero.

gobō [go·bo·o] Burdock, which has an artichoke-like flavor.

gohei [go·he·i] Wooden wands with zigzag white paper attached, used in Shinto ceremonies.

Heisei [he·i·se·i] The name of the current era, dating from Emperor Akihito's coronation on January 8, 1989.

hibakusha [hi·ba·ku·sha] Atomic bomb survivor.

hijiki [hi·ji·ki] A black sea-grass, often eaten with fish.

hinamatsuri [hi·na·ma·tsu·ri] The Dolls' Festival, celebrated on March 3rd.

hitodama [hi·to·da·ma] The souls of the just-departed, sometimes seen as flickering blue-green apparitions.

hotaru [ho·ta·ru] Fireflies, which have been used metaphorically in Japanese literature since the 8th century, often to suggest the ephemeral nature of life.

ikayaki [i·ka·ya·ki] Fried squid.

imagawayaki [i·ma·ga·wa·ya·ki] Waffles filled with *anko* paste.

jishin [ji·shin] Earthquake.

johakyu [jo·ha·kyu] The three parts of a Japanese musical composition: exposition, development, and resolution.

jyagabata [jiya·ga·ba·ta] Potatoes with butter and soy sauce.

kagura [ka·gu·ra] A performing art with both religious and folkloric traditions.

kagurabue [ka·gu·ra·bu·e] *kagura* flute.

kaki-kōri [ka·ki·ko·o·ri] Chipped ice with fruit syrup.

kami [ka·mi] Deity. The allusion to eight million *kami* is considered by scholars to have originally meant "a multitude" of *kami*.

kamiarizuki [ka·mi·a·ri·zu·ki] The month when all the gods are present.

kana [ka·na] The Japanese syllabary.

kanji [kan·ji] The Chinese characters adapted by the Japanese to write their native language.

kannazuki [kan·na·zu·ki] The month when all the gods are absent.

karaage [ka·ra·a·ge] Fried chicken.

keyaki [ke·ya·ki] An elm-like tree (*Zelkova serrata*).

kimono [ki·mo·no] A traditional Japanese garment.

kōban [ko·o·ban] A small neighborhood police station.

komainu [ko·ma·i·nu] A pair of lion-like figures placed on either side of a shrine's gate to ward off evil.

konbu [kon·bu] A type of kelp, used for soup stock.

konnichi-wa [kon·ni·chi·wa] Hello.

kotatsu [ko·ta·tsu] A low table covered by a futon.

koto [ko·to] A thirteen-stringed instrument with movable bridges.

kotsuzume [ko·tsu·zu·me] A drum whose two skins are stretched tight with a lacing of rope, and which is held by the musician at shoulder height and struck with fingers or palm.

ma [ma] A pause between musical notes that is used for dramatic effect.

manga [man·ga] Stories told using illustrated panels, in a comic-book fashion. The Japanese use *manga* across all genres, for serious topics as well as for entertainment.

matcha [ma·tcha] Finely milled green tea used in *chado* ceremonies.

matsuri [ma·tsu·ri] A festival of prayer and celebration.

matsutake [ma·tsu·ta·ke] A highly prized mushroom that grows under Japanese Red Pine trees.

mikoshi [mi·ko·shi] A palanquin used to parade a *kami* through the village.

miso [mi·so] A cooking paste made from fermented soybeans.

misogi [mi·so·gi] The use of water in a purification rite.

mitsuba [mi·tsu·ba] Wild parsley.

mochi [mo·chi] Rice that has been pounded into a paste.

mozuku [mo·zu·ku] A slippery dark-brown seaweed, served as a palate refresher.

mukaebi [mu·ka·e·bi] A small fire to beckon ancestral spirits.

noren [no·ren] Split curtain panels that allow easy passage into and out of a semi-private space.

nori [no·ri] Thin, dried seaweed, famously used in sushi.

obon-no-uta [o·bon·no·u·ta] The traditional song and dance performed at the opening and closing of the *obon* celebration.

ocha [o·cha] Green tea.

oden [o·den] Boiled vegetables and fish cakes.

odori [o·do·ri] Traditional Japanese folk songs and dances that have their verses and choreography adapted to fit local themes.

ofuro [o·fu·ro] A public bathhouse that is shared by hotel guests or neighborhood residents.

okedaiko [o·ke·da·i·ko] A large, lightweight drum, carried by the player in a sling, and played on both heads.

okinami [o·ki·na·mi] An immense sea wave.

okonomiyaki [o·ko·no·mi·ya·ki] Cabbage pancakes.

okuribi [o·ku·ri·bi] A small fire for releasing ancestral spirits from their earthly bonds.

omiyage [o·mi·ya·ge] Souvenirs meant to be given to friends upon return from travel, oftentimes they are local handicrafts or food specialties.

onigiri [o·ni·gi·ri] Rice balls. Cooked, short-grain rice, pressed into thick triangular shapes, that are easily carried.

onryo [on·ri·yo] Spirits that inhabit purgatory while awaiting resolution.

onsen [on·sen] Bathing springs.

origami [o·ri·ga·mi] Folded paper forms.

ramen [ra·men] Wheat noodles.

renkon [ren·kon] Lotus root.

ryokan [riyo·kan] A traditional Japanese inn with private rooms, but with shared bath and common eating room.

sake [sa·ke] A common alcoholic beverage brewed from rice.

sakoku [sa·ko·ku] The edict which restricted foreigners from visiting Japan, and prohibited citizens from leaving Japan.

satoimo [sa·to·i·mo] Taro root, like small sweet potatoes.

shamisen [sha·mi·sen] A three-stringed, banjo-like instrument that is plucked.

shiatsu [shi·a·tsu] A Japanese deep tissue massage.

shimedaiko [shi·me·da·i·ko] A small, tight-skinned *taiko*.

shimenawa [shi·me·na·wa] A sacred rope that wards off unclean spirits.

shinobue [shi·no·bu·e] A seven-holed bamboo flute.

shiso [shi·so] *Perilla frutescens*, a broadleaf plant often used for its mint-like flavor.

shoganai [sho·ga·na·i] An expression of acceptance for a situation that can't be changed.

shōji [sho·o·ji] Sliding doors constructed of a wooden lattice, and covered in *washi*.

shonanoka [sho·na·no·ka] The Buddhist rite offered on the seventh day, when the dead have fully departed from the earthly realm.

shoyu [sho·yu] Soy sauce.

soba [so·ba] Buckwheat noodles.

suzu [su·zu] Jingle bells on a handle-held stick.

tabi [ta·bi] Split-toed socks worn with or without sandals.

taiko [ta·i·ko] Traditional Japanese drum.

taisha [ta·i·sha] A grand shrine.

takama-no-hara [ta·ka·no·ga·ha·ra] The Plain of High Heaven, where the *kami* reside.

take [ta·ke] Bamboo shoots.

takoyaki [ta·ko·ya·ki] Fried octopus.

tanko-bushi [tan·ko·bu·shi] The coal miners' dance.

tatami [ta·ta·mi] The thick rice-straw mats used as flooring in many Japanese homes.

tate-eboshi [ta·te·e·bo·shi] A head covering worn by priests or performers during Shinto liturgical practices.

torii [to·ri·i] Tall gates constructed of two wooden pillars and a top plate (like the Greek letter π), used to delineate a shrine's sacred space.

tōrō nagashi [to·o·ro·o·na·ga·shi] The drifting away of the souls, a ceremony where lanterns are placed in a river to be carried to the sea.

tsunami [tsu·na·mi] A sequence of larger than normal ocean waves, triggered by a deep sea disturbance.

udon [u·don] Flour noodles.

ukiyoe [u·ki·yo·e] Japanese woodblock prints, literally "pictures of the floating world".

umeboshi [u·me·bo·shi] A small pickled plum, usually prepared with red *shiso* leaves that impart their color.

wagashi [wa·ga·shi] A confection made of rice and *anko*.

wakame [wa·ka·me] A green seaweed of subtle flavor, used in soups and salads.

warabi [wa·ra·bi] Fiddleheads. The furled fronds of a young fern.

washi [wa·shi] Handmade paper.

yagura [ya·gu·ra] A bandstand at the center of a dance area where the musicians play, and the master of ceremonies officiates.

yakiniku [ya·ki·ni·ku] Grilled beef.

yakitori [ya·ki·to·ri] Grilled chicken.

Yamata-no-Orochi [ya·ma·ta·no·o·ro·chi] The mythical serpent with eight heads and eight tails that was slain by *Susanō-no-mikoto*

yashiro [ya·shi·ro] A Shinto shrine.

yukata [yu·ka·ta] Light cotton *kimono*, normally worn indoors as pajamas, but also worn outdoors during summer festivals.

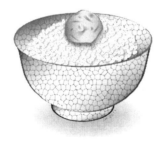

CPSIA information can be obtained at www.ICGtesting.com
Printed in the USA
BVOW080246270812

298727BV00003B/1/P